Walking with
IGNATIUS

ARTURO SOSA, SJ

SUPERIOR GENERAL OF THE SOCIETY OF JESUS

In Conversation with DARÍO MENOR

Prologue by SR. JOLANTA KAFKA, RMI

President of the International Union of Superiors General

Original title: *En camino con Ignacio,*
by Fr. Arturo Sosa, SJ, Superior General of the Society of Jesus–In
conversation with Darío Menor
© Curia Generalizia della Compagnia di Gesù, 2021
Published under an agreement with Grupo de Comunicación Loyola,
S. L. U. (Bilbao—Spain).

Translated by E.Twiston-Davies

Imprimatur:
✠ Manuel Sánchez Monge
Bishop of Santander
March 12, 2021

Photo credits
Cover: Cameron Casey, and courtesy of the Curia Generalizia della
Compagnia di Gesù.
Spine: Thomas Rochford, SJ, and JJ Mueller, SJ/Jesuits USA Central and
Southern Province.
Back cover: Robert Ballecer, SJ, 2019.
Author photos: Arturo Sosa, SJ, photo by © SJ-Bild/Céline Fossati, Darío
Menor photo courtesy of the Curia Generalizia della Compagnia di Gesù.

Unless otherwise noted, internal art is courtesy of the Curia Generalizia
della Compagnia di Gesù.

ISBN: 9781788124553

Printed by Hussar Books

Contents

Sr. Jolanta Kafka, RMI
President of the International Union
of Superiors General

Prologue

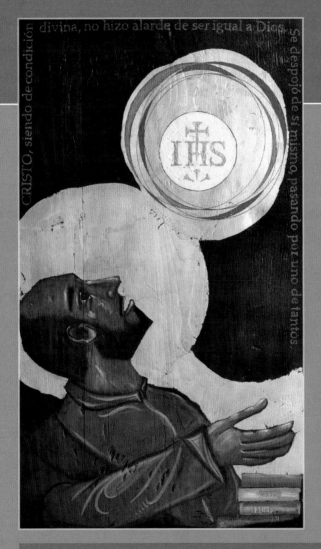

CRISTO, siendo de condición divina, no hizo alarde de ser igual a Dios. Se despojó de sí mismo, pasando por uno de tantos

Ignatius begging for alms to fund his studies.
Alejandro Labajos, SJ

To the Reader

1. The Beginning

I don't know if you have ever had the chance to visit the magnificent Church of Santa Maria del Mar in Barcelona. I have often been there retracing the steps of Father Claret, the founder of my congregation. Occasionally he preached there. But I also found another hidden treasure, one of several squirrelled away there. On the step of one of the last side chapels on the left, I found a small plaque. This was years ago, it was scarcely legible, but it said something along the lines of, "This is where St. Ignatius used to sit, begging for alms." Father Ignatius, here? In this corner of the Church? Begging for alms? I couldn't quite get my head round this. It certainly didn't fit with the mental image I had of St. Ignatius. But, yes, it was him alright. Ignatius had begged for alms to survive, to share among the poor, to fund his journey to Paris. This was during the pilgrim's first phase of conversion, as he sought ways to serve God and his Church: an experience of being stripped from the inside out, amid the poverty he shared with the poor, amid his dreams of studies that would shed light on his faith. In more recent times, a statue of St. Ignatius that expresses this inner emptying has been placed in the chapel. It speaks of his experience, of that internal need to make the self a passive space for God so as to find him, to follow him, to serve him in our brothers and sisters. If you ever have the chance to go, sit down next to that statue. Now see things from its perspective.

What went through Ignatius's heart on that step in Santa Maria del Mar, was the prelude to the birth of the Society of Jesus... Five hundred years have already passed since then.

You hold within your hands a book that celebrates the story of those events, and it's not only for the Ignatian family. Recalling the conversion of St. Ignatius can shed light on the consecrated life as a whole and be reason enough for us to start a new conversation about our presence and mission in the world. Ignatius's lodestar was a vast desire for God, for discovering his will, for following and serving him. The same has been true of the religious life since its very beginnings with monasticism and remained so ever since as is witnessed by the many, diverse forms of consecration that exist today. Every new charism is born of a similar foundational experience: unconditional openness to God, being emptied within, listening to him, and seeking him. After all, was not the phrase "the quest for God," *quaerere Deum*, how the consecrated life was described at its very beginning?

2. Questions

If the religious life is to continue walking in the fresh light of prophecy, it cannot stop searching. Nor can it tire of asking deep questions about the world, about God, its own existence and mission. "You know how to interpret the appearance of the sky, but you cannot interpret the signs of the times" (Mt. 16:3). For this, spiritual sensitivity is needed, the gleaning and sifting of questions so that they do not just remain theoretical. The times we are living in bombard us with questions: about the meaning of our consecration, about how we should live and what we should do, about how to pray, how to build fraternity, how to be with and close to the poorest of the poor, what we should hold onto, what we should let go of, who to involve in our quest and our discoveries... Where is God? Where are his prophets and prophetesses? "For both prophet and priest have gone roving about in the land that they do not know" (Jer. 14:18). If you have found that the answers to such questions don't come easily, then this book is for you... try to discern the answers, even if only partial, as you read. It is vital that you allow the questions to come up and don't ignore them.

What you will discover here is a kaleidoscope of questions. I hope you will be able to identify at least one that you are already mulling over, and grapple with the answer. Perhaps you may even find new questions and discover within them God's call, that he is awaiting your response. But of course, not everything will slot neatly into questions and answers.

3. Discernment

Pope Francis has asked the Society of Jesus to join him in helping discernment to flourish in the life of the Church. On the roadmap leading towards large-scale change, "discernment" is necessary. That was the teaching of St. Ignatius and the attitude to life embraced by the disciples of Jesus.

Perhaps the instability and the degree of confusion we are living through will accelerate processes of change: if our sense of being unsettled is great, if we are in the deepest watch of the night, are we not, in fact, closer to the dawn? Can we not embrace this path in our role as pilgrims of God rather than as those who dwell in his home? Just as with St. Ignatius, our own roadmap is shaped by discernment.

Among the many examples of questions and answers that have emerged at this time, two in particular spring to mind. One involves a Benedictine convent, which, given the restrictions on meetings and liturgical celebrations, asked itself the following: what do people need right now? What can we offer? What is God calling us to? After a time of colloquy among the sisters, they reached a decision. Via social media, they publicised their availability to accompany people, to listen, and to converse with them either online or via visits to the convent. They became open to welcoming people who needed to be listened to, without judgement. The convent parlour, it could be said, is now virtual, and has transformed into a place for encounter and caregiving. A young girl, speaking of her personal experience of this, said it made her joyful to discover that the nuns were so connected to daily life. This style of consecrated life appealed to her.

Now, I'll paint you another picture: a room where twenty volunteers, including lay people, believers, non-believers and a few consecrated religious, are preparing Christmas parcels for prisoners… This room has also become a meeting place, the expression of a Church that asks these kinds of questions, drawing people together so that they may serve the most needy in society.

You might ask whether this is just a temporary phenomenon or whether religious communities have already set their course and are joining humanity as it journeys towards new horizons of solidarity. Are they committed to travelling alongside others, drawing, just as Jesus taught us, on a shared vocation-mission of filiation and brotherhood?

As you walk with Ignatius, you will find that discernment requires religious life to be set down on that chapel step, so it can exist in humility close to the threshold of the altar, seeking and finding new forms of mission in the service of the Church. In the light of the many challenges of today, who, if not male and female religious, the followers of Jesus, can offer this freedom through discerning how to place themselves wholly in the hands of God to serve, without falling prey to ideology?

4. Together

Yes, conversation is worthwhile: being bold in seeking the answers and doing so together. This book is also a conversation, but behind the two main characters are dialogues and contributions from many others, both living and dead. While the subject of discernment is always the individual, at the same time, it is the community which flourishes if this dynamic is at work in the background. We need to discern. We need community.

Achieving both unity and complementarity in mission is one of our greatest challenges. How much envy and criticism of others lie behind that self-justifying plaint, "We can manage on our own"? This is the form of alms we must learn to beg for to-day on the doorstep of our houses and churches: the grace of depending more on others, of receiving wisdom, of waiting for diversity, for the arrival of many others, so that we can share what we have among us all.

Like me, I'm sure you will finish this book thanking Darío for each of the questions, which being both general and detailed, will lead you in different directions, and also Father Arturo for his answers, expressed with his typical depth, spirit, and kindness. You may also wish to thank God, who draws us into this dynamic of ever greater fidelity (*Magis*) that embraces our lives so completely, allowing us to join the path of Ignatius, in the footsteps of Jesus.

Finally, as you begin reading, I leave you, as words of guidance, this prayer of St. Ignatius taken from the Spiritual Exercises. It is the best way to feel that you are in his presence as, led by his spirit, you wander through these pages.

Take, Lord, and receive all my liberty,
my memory, my understanding,
and my entire will,

All I have and call my own.
You have given all to me.
To you, Lord, I return it.

Everything is yours; do with it what you will.
Give me only your love and your grace,
that is enough for me.

Introduction

A Hopeful Future

Child at a school in a JRS camp in Chad
Don Doll, SJ – Creighton University

For me, this book has meant a leap into an adventure. I hope that it will also be an adventure for you, the reader.

Start to read it wherever you like. Pause whenever you find good fruit, sense the presence of the Lord, and become aware of his voice. For you, this book could prove the start of a journey towards a new way of finding God or hearing his voice in your life. This isn't an erudite spiritual or sociological work. It is rather an invitation to "realise and relish things interiorly" (*Spiritual Exercises, 2*). This book, in short, aims to help you grow, starting in the exact place you find yourself in, guided by the Lord and advancing step by step.

You will find in these pages reflections about the world of today, the Church, and the Society of Jesus, with a strong emphasis on the Universal Apostolic Preferences, alongside a few suggestions for reflection and prayer. They are there to invite you to become a pilgrim yourself so that you may walk the path of Christian adventure in our changing world.

After he was wounded in Pamplona in 1521, Ignatius of Loyola became a pilgrim, being guided by the Lord himself. The title of this book, *Walking with Ignatius*, is an invitation to explore the path he followed, so that we too may become pilgrims and set off, allowing ourselves to be guided by the Spirit. It is also an invitation to be open to the grace that will purify our gaze, so that we can see ourselves, other people, and nature with the eyes of the Lord. God sees with eyes of love, mercy, and hope, and his gaze renews the world. United to him, we will discover, through his grace,

God sees with eyes of love, mercy, and hope.

his loving presence throughout history and confirm our commitment to the care of creation (*Ex*, 235–237).

Exploring the process that led Ignatius of Loyola to completely transform his life and outlook can help us examine whether our own processes of conversion—at a personal, community, and institutional level—are opening us up to the newness of a future filled with hope. It is my hope that these pages may help us reach the full depth of our examen, as individuals and as groups.

That battle in Pamplona that left Ignatius wounded was the catalyst for his process of conversion. A new light then led him to understand afresh himself and his mission in this world. His petty dreams of fame and fortune were shattered, his fantasies lay in ruins at his feet. But the Lord offered Ignatius new ideals, dreams, and hopes, which led him to set out on paths very different to those that, in his poverty, he had once dreamt of.

This can also happen to us. Perhaps life is pushing us, gently or painfully, to abandon the little dreams we once had for our lives, so that we may enter the energy of *magis*. This dynamic leads us to accept God's invitation to unite ourselves to his dream of human fraternity.

> **The Lord invites us to share his dream for the world.**

This isn't about doing more, or our natural leaning towards activism. It is rather that the Lord invites us to share his dream for the world, promising to sustain us on this shared adventure.

A book like this is obviously the result of teamwork. All those involved have kept the focus constantly on you, the reader. We have tried to share my points of view in a straightforward fashion, yet with the greatest possible respect for the culture, calling, and life journey of each of our readers. I hope we have succeeded.

The book is the fruit of a series of well-prepared interviews and never would have happened without the generous help of Darío Menor. For two and half months, we met up week after week for the interviews. His stimulating questions, patient listening, and professionalism as he grasped the meaning of my thoughts and committed them to paper were vital to the success of this project. Many thanks!

I would also like to express my gratitude for the help, competent support, and advice of my companions in the General Curia of the Society to Jesus, in particular to José María Bernal, John Dardis, Antoine Kerhuel, and Jesús Zaglul. I also thank Pierre Bélanger for his valuable suggestions regarding photographs and images. Cristian Peralta wrote the prayers that close each chapter and comprise an invitation to go deeper, both as individuals and communities, into the topics addressed in each part of the book. Yet without the help of Ramón Alfonso Díez Aragón and the team at Grupo de Comunicación Loyola in Spain, the book in your hands right now would never have seen the light of day.

It is my hope that everyone who reads this book may feel like a pilgrim in the process. Preparing it has been a grace for me personally and has helped me to broaden my horizons. I hope it will also help you, dear reader, to see the world around you, the Church, the Society of Jesus, and your own life with fresh eyes. For that is the key to every journey of renewal.

I dedicate this book to the members of the apostolic body of the Society of Jesus across the world, but in particular to those of the province of Venezuela. Among them I have found over many years all the support I have needed in my journey as a Jesuit: from them I have received just the right *cura apostolica* and *cura personalis* required at every moment. They gave me, in turn, invaluable opportunities to give back what I had received.

During my time as Father General I have visited many countries and different continents. I have met in equal measure Jesuits and companions, male and female, on the mission who face situations of darkness and danger every day. All of them are people who place their hands in those of Jesus. Their trust amazes me. Their love, their hope and fidelity console me. This book is a small token of gratitude for all the Jesuits in the world and also for those, both male and female, who are our companions on the mission. Let us go forth together, *in nomine Domini*, placing our trust in the one who calls us and who is faithful.

Arturo Sosa, SJ

Father General of the Society of Jesus

Rome, January 2021

Five hundred years ago, on May 20th, 1521, Íñigo López de Loyola was wounded in a battle in Pamplona. As his leg was hit by a cannon ball, his dreams of fame and fortune were smashed to smithereens. During a long convalescence, he learnt to see the world with fresh eyes: his encounter with Christ changed his life.

1 St. Ignatius of Loyola: Becoming a Pilgrim

Saint Ignatius Loyola. Oil painting by Monserrat Gudiol at the cave in Manresa.

In your opinion, what is St. Ignatius's greatest contribution to the Church and to society in general?

The universal and long-term nature of his vision. He was able to see beyond immediate events and look forward in time. Today, we'd call that having strategic vision. Ignatius's ability to do this was intimately linked to his experience of God. He knew how to forget himself so that he could see everything from the perspective of the Trinity. Ignatius truly became "Catholic," no easy feat as it involves adopting a long-term universal outlook, encompassing the whole of humankind.

Experiencing God does not limit you. Instead he widens your understanding of yourself, of humanity, and of history. Ignatius's universal vision became the basic criteria for the discernment process that precedes decision making in the Society of Jesus, as it seeks continually to render greater and better service to the Church and the world. This always involves choosing the greatest universal good. This approach is, I think, a huge contribution from Ignatius.

> **Experiencing God does not limit you. Instead, he widens your understanding of yourself, of humanity, and of history.**

What can Catholics today learn from the person of Ignatius and emulate, in particular, from his process of conversion?

How to become Catholics. We should not assume someone is Catholic just because they have been baptised. Baptism is a sacrament, desired by the adult who receives it or by the parents or Godparents when the person to be baptised is a child. It marks the starting point of a process which must continue, as we allow ourselves to be profoundly transformed and shift our focus away from self and towards others. The key is to put Jesus at the centre. This cannot be separated from our mission.

That was the process undertaken by Ignatius, who suggested a style of religious life in which communal living was founded on fraternal communication rather than being shaped by the walls of a monastery or by living under the same roof. This was a type of lifestyle for religious quite different from that which had prevailed previously. Ignatius used the phrase, "friends in the Lord," which reveals the centrality of the Eucharist and the importance of communication in the life of the Society of Jesus. Both were essential for the creation of this body, which offers a fundamentally apostolic style of consecration, at whose heart is prayer.

Jerónimo Nadal, in his analysis of Ignatius, said that we needed to be contemplatives in action, able to find the Lord in our daily lives. That's the basis for our activities never being confined to one sphere. Any activity that helps make the Word of Jesus present is valid for a Jesuit religious.

In your opinion, which is the key Ignatian text? The Spiritual Exercises? The Constitutions? Or something else?

To a reader who knows nothing about Ignatius I'd give the *Autobiography*, which is fascinating. He didn't want to write it, but eventually gave in to his companions' requests. He was already an old man when he ended up dictating this account of his life. The *Autobiography* is an examen of his life, in which

Ignatius relays God's action throughout his life, in the form of an examen. Then there are his *Letters*, which provide endless information about the practical decisions taken in the Society, which was then being founded and in a phase of growth. They sketch out how the Society functioned, up until the writing of the *Constitutions*, another amazing text.

After the Pope had approved the *Formula of the Institute*, a relatively brief declaration of intent, the Society began to grow. That was why Ignatius's companions asked him to write the *Constitutions*. Initially, he was not convinced of the need for this because he maintained that the Society should have enough spiritual energy to govern itself, depending on the degree to which each Jesuit fully lived out his charism, without requiring a regulatory framework. It took him quite a while to prepare the *Constitutions*, but after a process of discernment he managed to present a very original framework for a rule of religious intimately linked to his spiritual experience. Nearly five centuries later, it remains an inspirational text for the Jesuit community.

He was also reluctant to write the Spiritual Exercises. Why was that?

Ignatius was no writer. He wrote only when he had no other alternative. The Spiritual Exercises are notes reflecting his experience, but if you give them to someone without an explanatory guide, they won't make it past page five. Ignatius wrote because he wanted to communicate. He wanted to speak to people about God and present them with a spiritual experience, but he also had to communicate with his brethren and others: benefactors, monarchs, and those who helped him to found a school. He maintained this network of relationships from a room that you can still visit in the Gesù in Rome. It is striking to think of someone with delicate health, enclosed there for so many years, yet who found the energy to achieve all that he did. Another significant, although little-known work by Ignatius is his *Spiritual Diary*. These were notes that he made about what he sensed spiritually during a specific time of his life. They are a practical example of his spiritual discernment.

Would Ignatius's conversion have happened at all without the trauma of his wound in Pamplona?

Who knows what might have happened if he had not been wounded. Whatever the case, in the life of any individual there are many instances that offer us the chance to open up to the transcendent, as happened in the conversion of Ignatius. For him, it all began as he recovered from his wound, but similar experiences can arise in other contexts, e.g., being in lockdown, in prison, going travelling, or facing the unknown. There are times in life that shake you up and kick-start this process. In Scripture, we have the example of St. Paul, who fell to the ground, heard the voice of Jesus, and was temporarily blind, and Peter, for whom the cock crowing opened up a new way to love and follow the Lord, or Zacchaeus, who climbed up a tree to see Jesus.

In any case, conversion never really happens in one fell swoop but is really a life-long process. Ignatius, for instance, never saw himself as having converted but as being a pilgrim. He never believed that he'd reached his goal. Christian life is a pilgrimage in which you put aside your plans to set out on a journey, allowing yourself to be guided, accompanied, open to surprises. However much of a strategic vision you have, you can never totally control your life if you're really open to being guided by the Spirit.

There is one particular moment in the conversion of St. Ignatius which I find striking. While he was on the way to Montserrat, he met a Muslim who said he didn't believe in the virginity of Mary. Ignatius wondered afterwards whether he should let the Muslim go or follow him and kill him. He left the decision to the direction taken by his donkey, according to whether the animal led him along the road to the village where the Muslim had gone or in another direction. How do you interpret this incident referred to in the Autobiography?

This happened at a point where Ignatius was beginning to recognise his interior movements, and no longer gave in automatically to his instincts, which previously would have led him without any hesitation to kill the Muslim. His cultural and family baggage and knightly training pushed him to not allow anyone to insult Our Lady. But here Ignatius, who must have been a very impulsive kind of man, managed to control himself by drawing on his faith: he considered what he should do and turned to another creature—in this instance, the donkey, as he was on the road and had no other companion. This scene reveals his conversion process at a very early stage.

Ignatius went through very deep and at times very long crises during his conversion process. What did he learn from them? How do you interpret the temptation to commit suicide that he felt at one point?

The greatest temptation for any human being is to take their own life rather than surrender it. Suicide is the greatest act of taking one's own life any individual can take consciously and freely, as though saying, "My life is mine to the point where I'll kill myself." Today, however, we know that the vast majority of suicides are caused by profound states of depression, in which an individual loses all self-control. In contrast, if you give your life to another, you shift your focus outwards. That other person might kill you, but it will be because you are freely giving them your life. That doesn't prevent you going through deep crises, which are part of the interior life. The transformation that conversion involves can't be experienced without times of deep crisis, as the Gospels demonstrate. In this context, the most dramatic depiction of this is the agony in the garden where Jesus completely abandons what Ignatius might well have described as "his self-love, will, and interest." Everyone faces crises that can be understood in spiritual or psychological terms, in which the greatest temptation may be to take one's own life. This is something that is so much part of contemporary culture and reveals its limitations.

> **The transformation that conversion involves can't be experienced without times of deep crisis.**

Have you ever been through this kind of crisis?

I've never felt like throwing myself out of a window, but I have certainly been through those times of crisis when you think, "What am I doing here?" These are crises about meaning, which relates to faith and the choices you've made in life. It's hard when you question the big decisions and can't see any meaning in your life choices. But these can also be times of validation. What is the Cross? It's the moment when you ask yourself if the path you've chosen makes any sense. The key thing is how you come out of the crisis and if you validate the decisions you have taken previously.

During his time in Manresa, Ignatius underwent a mysterious experience by the banks of the Cardoner River. It wasn't a vision but he insisted that there he learnt much about the faith and the world and left with the clear objective of helping souls. How do you understand this incident? Did it shape in some way Ignatius's life and the future of the Society?

I understand this as a very normal human experience. We go through processes until we reach a new state of consciousness. There are times when we become aware of what we've been going through previously via our experiences, relationships, or reading. Those moments are like when suddenly you're able to put everything together like the pieces in a jigsaw puzzle, or as happened to Ignatius near the Cardoner River, everything comes together through the grace of God. This can occur in small or large matters.

This brings to mind something that happened to me, and that, details aside, may help to explain this. I was in charge of moving the Gumilla Centre in Caracas into a much smaller building. It looked like it wouldn't fit into the smaller building, but one day I woke at 3 a.m. and, sprawling out on the floor, sketched out on a piece of paper how we could resolve the problem. Perhaps that's a silly example, but it does illustrate what happens sometimes when the pieces randomly fit together and complex processes become easy to understand. Something similar happened in regard to my understanding of my country's journey through history. After many experiences, much reading, and many conversations... at a particular point in time, I suddenly "got" the process. What Ignatius experienced by the banks of the Cardoner was something similar. Previously, he'd felt, heard, and experienced things randomly, but it was only there that he managed to make sense of and finally grasp the whole picture. Some situations take time for us to fully understand. It's a bit like what happens when you are making a recipe. Making *sancocho*, for example (a popular beef stew dish in Latin America), might seem easy, but each of the ingredients requires a different cooking time, and if the preparation is not right, the result won't be good. God and his action within us also take time.

Although spiritual discernment is a core element of Ignatius's process, as the Exercises and the basic decision-making process of the Society make clear, it wasn't something he invented. What did Ignatius learn about discernment from the Church's existing tradition and what did he contribute to it?

Unlike many other Christians, Ignatius took seriously the idea that receiving the Holy Spirit was crucial. We should trust in the Holy Spirit's presence alongside us throughout our lives. For Ignatius, Jesus was to be followed through discernment, in the presence of the Holy Spirit. When someone sets out on the Christian journey, they don't know where they will end up. The answer lies in Pentecost, without which neither the Church nor the Christian life would exist. Jesus promised us he would be with us always, through the Holy Spirit, until the end of the world. That is what Ignatius received and worked on. He was able to perceive how the Spirit moved both in his own life and in the lives of others. That is why he devised rules for spiritual discernment to help others do this. But the rules are not an instruction manual. They are a light to guide us so we may perceive whatever it is we need to experience.

At what point do you perceive God's presence most strongly in the life of Ignatius? Is it possible for everyone to understand his visions and mystical experiences?

I'm sure they were hard for Ignatius to understand too. Some experiences can be spoken of long only after they occur, when you understand them or they no longer harm you. With mystical experiences, things are even more complicated because they are always bewildering. Ignatius was striving to find God in all things. That's how his daily life gradually filled with God, but not in an artificial way. It was rather that, bit by bit, he began encountering the Lord, in prayer and in the Eucharist of course, but also through his work and community life. That is the mysticism of St. Ignatius: not raptures that sweep you up and away from everyday living, but a sensitivity to finding God in all things.

The young Íñigo grew up without a mother. Did this shape his character? Did he seek in some way a maternal figure by choosing a Marian monastery like Montserrat as the key place for his conversion? How was Ignatius influenced by his devotion to Our Lady?

I don't see myself as an expert on the psyche of Ignatius or in fact of anybody else so I can't judge whether one's infancy shapes one's life. Psychologists place great store on this. However, I don't believe that devotion to Mary is necessarily about having a maternal substitute. I have a great devotion to Our Lady and it was, in fact, my mother and grandmothers who instilled this in me. The presence of Mary was as decisive in the life of Jesus as in the life of the first Christian community. Marian devotion was part of the environment Ignatius was born into and grew up in because it was very much part of popular Basque and Spanish religiosity. Experience of God leads us to an understanding of the ways in which he communicates with human beings: Mary is his great mediator. Devotion to Mary plays a key role in Christian life. Ignatius understood his own devotion to God to be connected to the Virgin Mary, as is abundantly clear in his *Autobiography*. He had a great devotion, for instance, to Our Lady of La Estrada whose statue was near him in the Gesù. In the Spiritual Exercises, Ignatius suggests that the retreatant should ask Mary in the colloquies to bring him or her to her son. Mary is a companion, a conduit to God.

Ignatius is depicted in his biographies as a dry Basque, restrained yet forthright. How much did his background influence his character?

It certainly did have an influence. I belong to one of the first generations of Venezuelans in the Society's Venezuelan province, so had the chance to meet many of its founders who were Basques and men of Navarre and Aragon. We used to joke, I remember, that my inculturation as a Jesuit had happened via the Basque Country. I agree that first impressions of the Basques suggest that they are tough, but then you discover their gentleness. They're a bit like rustic bread, which has a hard crust but is very sweet inside and seasoned with great feeling. Ignatius was certainly influenced by his background, for example, in his writing, which can come across as very concise and dry but conceals a beautiful sensitivity that can help the reader to develop an inner tenderness. Without doubt, Ignatius was the product of his time, his family, and his cultural entourage.

The Society of Jesus owes a great deal to the Basques. As well as Ignatius and Arrupe, a large number of Jesuits from the Basque country travelled all over the world. I learnt a great deal from the Basque Jesuit brothers in Venezuela when I was young. Then it was the rule that the brothers could not study so they learnt Spanish in the Society by hearing it. As their maternal tongue was Basque, it was sometimes quite funny to hear them speak in Spanish. I became great friends with a Jesuit brother, José Manuel Salegui, who had been a shepherd. He never quite mastered Spanish, but he talked to everyone and had an impressive ability to listen to others and to communicate in depth. It was a great help for the Society that

Ignatius was Basque, although the origins of that initial group of Jesuits were very diverse.

St. Ignatius was not ordained a priest until he was forty-seven years old. What do you make of the fact that he did not take this step any earlier?

What developed in St. Ignatius from his conversion onwards was a great apostolic vocation, which at the beginning was not linked to the priesthood. So much was this the case that he began his work without being either a priest or a religious. He started to talk to people, to offer the Spiritual Exercises, to preach the Word, and to do good. As his vocation to serve others developed, the need to be a priest arose almost as an afterthought. After surviving hardships including imprisonment, persecution, and being regarded with suspicion, Ignatius saw ordination to the priesthood as an appropriate way to fulfill his apostolic vocation. It's important to remember that priesthood in the Society bears this hallmark: this is a group united above all by its apostolic vocation and not only by the sacrament of priestly ordination. The vocation of a Jesuit brother is as apostolic as that of a Jesuit priest. The priesthood is lived out in the Society of Jesus as an apostolic instrument, not as a means to attain privilege.

Do you think it is fitting to view Ignatius as an apostle of the Counter-Reformation?

To me, the idea of the Reformation and the Counter-Reformation feels like a straitjacket that can lead to a multi-coloured story being seen only in black and white. I don't find this particularly helpful, because I see Ignatius as a great reformer. He promoted a profound reformation of the Church by drawing on his particular spiritual experience. While Luther suggested a reformation that ended up with a schism he did not initially desire, in the Catholic Church we find reformers such as Francis of Assisi, Ignatius of Loyola, St. John of the Cross, St. Teresa of Avila, St. Teresa of Lisieux, and St. Philip Neri, and so many others, many of whom are saints who founded religious congregations. They obtained reforms without causing division. They differed from Luther in how they expressed their desire for reform in the Church. Ignatius never placed himself above the Church but beneath it. I am not judging Luther, but he challenged the structures of the Church. Ignatius, in contrast, understood that reform should start first with ourselves so that we may be at the service of the Church. His starting point was fidelity to the Church. When the story of Ignatius is looked at free of the clichés surrounding the Reformation and Counter-Reformation, his contribution to his time may be better understood.

What lessons can be learnt from the historical context in which St. Ignatius of Loyola lived and his activity at the time that might facilitate change today?

In Ignatius's day, different ways of understanding power co-existed, either from a perspective of freedom or one of imposition. Ignatius experienced this dilemma in his own life. He received his formation at court, but his transformation led him away from that path, to seek instead an alternative understanding of power. From the time he was consecrated as a religious, he was committed to empowering people to take part in public life. His experience leads me to dream of a world in which people contribute to the common good, from a place of responsible freedom. That is what the Society of Jesus is trying to foster.

Another Basque of universal renown, Miguel de Unamuno compared Ignatius to Don Quixote.[1] Do you think this is accurate? If so, who were the giants Ignatius believed he had to fight but which turned out to be windmills?

Let's not forget that Don Quixote is imaginary while Ignatius really existed. The comparison works, however, if you think that Cervantes presents Quixote as someone who pursues his dreams undaunted by obstacles. Ignatius was bold and pursued a dream that seemed impossible to many, and even to himself at some point. He did not fight against windmills but against real enemies and the giants nestling within him. He faced a significant internal battle. This was the origin of his skill for discernment and his offering a method to enable others to do likewise. The first obvious level of this battle was in the personal crisis he went through, while the second was posed by the Church in his clash with the giants in the Christian community of the day, who found it hard to be open towards the new way of understanding the religious life and apostolic priesthood presented by Ignatius. The third battle lay in his own life story. Ignatius left a tremendous legacy bearing the imprint of his DNA in the soul of individuals, in the Church and in history. We need to know how to find ourselves quixotically, within each of those three levels, fully aware that we're perceiving a dream that derives from

---

1   M. de Unamuno, *Our Lord Don Quixote: The life of Don Quixote and Sancho with related essays*, Routledge & K. Paul (1 Jan. 1967).

the Gospel and the inspiration of the Holy Spirit. This way of understanding the Christian life on three levels, beginning with inner experience, attracted me deeply when I was young to the character of Ignatius.

As well as the **Autobiography,** *there are numerous biographies of St. Ignatius. Which one do you think is the most accurate? Which one has helped you the most?*

One book which has influenced me and helped me understand Ignatius a lot better is *Ignacio de Loyola, solo y a pie,* by José Ignacio Tellechea Idígoras.[2] Other more recent books about him are equally good. For instance, I was also fascinated in quite a different way by *Heroic Leadership: Best Practices from a 450 Year Old Company That Changed the World* by Chris Lowney, an American who became an investment banker after several years as a Jesuit scholastic. It's an attempt to put the organisational method devised by Ignatius into the language of management. It caught my eye because to my mind the method Ignatius devised to organise the Society is terrific. It is something I'm very aware of as the Superior General.

It's astonishing because this is an institution that functions on the basis of full trust in every individual, a deep knowledge of individual members, and in-depth communication with decision makers. It's very flexible and has nothing in common with the image held of Jesuits being like soldiers. A soldier is never asked what he thinks. He carries out the orders he is given, exactly how he is told to. Just the opposite happens with

---

2   José Ignacio Tellechea Idígoras and Cornelius Michael Buckley, *Ignatius of Loyola: the Pilgrim Saint* (Chicago, IL: Loyola University Press, 1994).

a Jesuit: before taking action, he must first reflect and discern. The Society functions on the basis of knowing its members in order to send them where they will be best placed to yield the greatest apostolic fruit. Furthermore, our ultimate authority is not one individual but an assembly, the General Congregation, which delegates to the Superior General the authority required to ensure that the structures work, but he is obliged to consult others. This model is then replicated in the Society's different entities. No superior can dispense with consultation when making decisions.

Is there anything in St. Ignatius's journey that has not been part of your own experience?

Ignatius had his own journey, which I take as my reference point and source of inspiration. I find it helpful to ask myself what Ignatius would do in particular circumstances. Then I accept my own responsibility for whatever situation I find myself in. It also inspires me to see how Ignatius responded to his own individual, historic circumstances, while being at the same time aware that those I face are different. I also find it helpful to ask myself what Jesus would do in the situation I'm facing, knowing that his Holy Spirit is with me, just as he promised. Human life is very varied. I am very strongly of the opinion that everyone is responsible for his or her own life. Jesus shows us that the way to take responsibility for our lives is to forget ourselves and put our neighbour at the centre. This responsibility leads us to place ourselves in the hands of God. That's why discernment is so necessary.

What can be learned from Ignatius's way of exercising leadership? And from his ability to transform his personal conversion into an institution?

For me right now the biggest challenge is adapting the insights of Ignatius about the organisation of the Society to the circumstances of today. It's exciting to adjust these structures to bring new life to the institution today, through the judicious use of their flexibility and methods of delegating and communicating. The key ingredient, although this is sometimes lost sight of, is trust in each individual. Without trust and transparent communication, there would be no Society of Jesus. This should be present as much among Jesuits as in our relationships with non-Jesuits.

Which of the first companions of St. Ignatius appeals to you the most?

I must confess that I know considerably less about the earliest companions of Ignatius than about him. When we consider the history of the Society, perhaps we tend to forget a little about that initial group, which had a very important role, although of late, that imbalance has been a little more redressed. Each had their peculiarities. Pierre Favre, for example, was renowned as the companion who was best at giving the Spiritual Exercises and was a great traveler, roaming through Europe with ease. Then there was the youngest companion, Nicolás de Bobadilla, who was very bold and who felt responsible for the mission and began to open it up in new directions. What strikes me about Francis Xavier was his willingness. Initially, he was not assigned to go to India, but the one who was due to go fell ill so he offered to go instead. Without them, and without other companions such as Laínez, Salmerón, Simón Rodríguez, Jayo, Broët, Codure, Nadal, Polanco, Ribadeneira or Luis González de Cámara, St. Ignatius would never have become who he became. He managed to be the glue that held together a very diverse group of people. They were not a group of friends who founded a congregation, but individuals of differing ages and life journeys who became friends on their spiritual journey until together they founded the Society of Jesus.

Which other Jesuit saints do you think we should be more aware of today?

Fortunately, across more than four centuries of history in the Society, we have plenty to choose from. Many are recognised as Saints or are beatified. They are Jesuits of all ages and all walks of life, some being bolder and more missionary by nature than others. At this point in time, it's important to emphasise the lives of holy Jesuit brothers because we need to give greater emphasis to that vocation. The lives of some young Jesuits have also proved very inspiring, as is true of our martyrs who always hold a special appeal, regardless of whether they are long dead or have died more recently.

"THEY GRADUALLY REALISED FROM THE OUTSIDE THE CHANGE THAT HAD BEEN MADE INWARDLY IN HIS SOUL." [AU 10]

The first impression one gleans from the Shrine of Loyola in the Basque Country in Spain is that it was once home to a great and historic hero. The basilica rises up imposingly in the middle of the valley in contrast to the farmsteads so typical of the region. The high altar, with its marble altarpiece and fine inlays, is presided over by a magnificent statue of St. Ignatius, appearing triumphant and glorious. The side altars, the organ, and ornate dome bestow on the whole a note of solemn grandiosity. But, to the surprise of visitors, the guides who show them around the shrine never fail to invite them, as they leave the basilica, to see its "jewel." Passing through a side door marked "the holy house," they enter the discreet, austere house concealed by the vast architecture of the shrine, where St. Ignatius was born. And there it is, invisible from the outside yet nourishing the shrine's very soul. Half built of stone and half from brick, a consequence of futile battles, it begins to narrate a less glorious story. The next thing the visitor will see is a statue showing a wounded, failing Ignatius. Going up the stairs, one sees a depiction of his wild youth and his protector's fall from grace... Further up still are the family quarters and the memory of the mother we are not sure Ignatius ever knew... finally on the top floor we arrive at the rooms of the children of the family, where the "chapel of conversion" is found: an austere, simple, serene place which testifies to the passage of God through the life of this wounded man, who reposed there, entertained in between his knightly fantasies by reading the life of Christ and those of the saints. The "jewel of the place" reminds us who is guiding us. Above the altar is an inscription in Basque and Spanish that reads: "Here, Íñigo de Loyola gave himself to God." Here lies its value. In this discreet spot, God began to open a path in the heart of a wounded man, thus beginning the process of conversion which has touched the lives of so many.

PRAYER POINTS

The composition of place. Think of people you know who have experienced, despite their wounds or because of them, the Lord's invitation and call to fullness of life.

Grace to ask for. Lord, give me a courageous and open outlook so that I may recognise you at work in my life and in the life of many others.

First point. Dwell on experiences of conversion, whether small or large, in your personal faith story.

BIBLE TEXTS

» **Ephesians 1:3–14.** What do you feel when you read that you are loved prior to any effort or merit on your part? And what if the purpose of your life were to offer to the world the love you have received freely? What would this change for you? Where would you focus your efforts on a daily basis?

» **Jeremiah 18:1–6.** The invitation of the prophet Jeremiah is to allow ourselves to be moulded by the Lord. How do you cope with times of vulnerability? Do they become times when you turn inwards, or do they stir up a longing to trust others? Which of your experiences of God have helped you grow in trust with him?

» **Luke 5:1–11.** "Go away from me, Lord; I am a sinful man!" Those were the words of Peter to Jesus after the miraculous catch of fish. Jesus invited Peter to be a "fisher of men." Are you willing to hear the Lord's invitations? What is he inviting you to do? What have been the fruits of allowing yourself to be led by him in times of despair?

Colloquy. Speak to Mary, tell her about the desires and longings you have in your personal process of faith and ask her to obtain for you the grace from her Son so that you may grow in trust regarding his call and invitations. Finish with an Our Father and a Hail Mary. Do not forgot to examine what you have experienced during the prayer time.

TIPS FOR SPIRITUAL CONVERSATION

For spiritual conversation starting with personal prayer, the following steps from the general methodology of spiritual conversation are recommended (p. 268).

For spiritual conversation concerning an apostolic work, the following prayer points may be beneficial:

Composition of place. Consider the history of the apostolic work, its priorities and highlights, its shadows and challenges.

Grace to ask for. Lord, grant me a loving outlook, open to life and merciful with failings in regard to the apostolic work I am helping with. Grant me too the clarity to understand the invitation to conversation you offer us.

Bible texts. Jeremiah 18:1–6 / Ps 127 (126) 1–5: What processes of conversion is the Lord calling me to within the apostolic work to which I offer my gifts? Where is the Lord inviting us to walk?

Colloquy. Speak to Mary, tell her of the desires and longings that you have for this apostolic work. Ask her to obtain for you the grace of her son so that you may grow in trust regarding his call and invitations. Finish with an Our Father and a Hail Mary. Do not forget to examine what you have experienced during the prayer time. The fruits of this time may be shared, in accordance with the steps of general methodology for Spiritual Conversation.

Fr. Arturo Sosa was elected the Superior General of the Society of Jesus in October 2016. Born in Venezuela, he received his theological formation in Rome and has a broad experience of social and political sciences. He is the first successor of St. Ignatius of Loyola from Latin America.

2 Arturo Sosa: A Pilgrim Today

Be Seen. Daniel Leblond, SJ (Photo: M. Dubreuil)

If the young Arturo Sosa met you today, do you think he would be satisfied?

I think he would say "Well done" to me because I have done what I have enjoyed and that has made me happy. And yet I once dreamt of being a doctor because I loved biology and anatomy. I spent my time opening up animals like frogs and rats. I even owned a collection of spiders, which completely terrified my mother. If I put it in front of my bedroom door, she wouldn't come in. But what finished off my calling to medicine was the discovery that I fainted whenever I saw blood. So by the end of high school, I no longer had that dream, and a vocation as a Jesuit, which was always linked for me to social and political issues, the reality of my country, and the chance to serve those in the greatest need, attracted me more.

What was your relationship like with your parents and close family?

I grew up in an extended family. I'm the eldest of six siblings: four girls and two boys. Until I was 10 years old, we lived in the house of my maternal grandfather in Caracas, but we always had a close relationship with my paternal grandparents. Then my father and one of his brothers bought some land together and built two houses next door to each other, with a shared garden. My uncle and aunt also had six children, so it was really like a permanent party. We were also close to our neighbours and friends. Those were the days when you could walk freely through the streets of Caracas.

What did your parents do for work?

My father was the first person in his family to get a university degree, in law and economy. Then he worked for a group of businesses and created his own finance company. I used to say that this was down to me because he set it up the year I was born. He worked hard but also spent time at home. We had a really good relationship, and I often accompanied him on his travels through Venezuela, which was my first exposure to the country as a whole. I also had a very good relationship with my mother, who never finished high school as, due to a revolt in Venezuela, she wasn't able to take her exams. Later on, she married and devoted herself to her children.

I always felt very free: we were brought up to take personal responsibility and enjoy the freedom that goes with that. My parents encouraged us to invite friends home rather than having us go out on our own. I recall that we used to talk a fair bit and our grandparents were very much part of that. We would chat, above all with my grandfather Arturo, who was paralysed due to polio and was a great conversationalist.

Where does your interest in the political and social life of Venezuela come from?

Almost certainly through my father, who was quite involved in the world of politics. When I was 10 years old, the military dictatorship fell: he was named a minister and later a member of the governing junta that organised democratic elections. In the years prior to this, those who opposed the dictatorship would gather in secret at my house. Since I was very little, I began to hear at home many conversations about politics, although it was only later that I had a framework that allowed me to understand the whole context. My father was heavily criticised by his friends when he accepted the post of minister because they told him he was treading on stony ground, which would only yield trouble. He replied that it was impossible for his family to be ok if the country was doing badly and that he should make a contribution. He thought that you shouldn't try to live in a bubble.

Your first contact with the Society of Jesus was while you were a pupil at the Colegio San Ignacio in Caracas. What was that period in your life like?

My father had been at the school, although my mother's family was linked to the Sisters of St. Joseph of Tarbes and the De la Salle Brothers, who had educated my uncles. In those days, school filled up almost all our time, to the point where my father asked me as a joke if I lived at school or at home. As well as our classes and other activities, I remember that on the weekends we would visit the paediatric hospital of the Brothers of St. John of God to play with the children who were patients there. This made a real impression on me. Later on, we began to visit parts of Caracas, and during the holidays we took part in the work camps held in various parts of the country.

I was struck by the friendliness and goodness of the Jesuit brothers at the school. That was the starting point for my vocation. Some of them were teachers. Others were in charge of maintenance and other areas. The vast majority of those Jesuits were Basques or from Navarre, because those sent to Venezuela belonged to the Society's Spanish province. I really liked the way that the brothers related to us and to the world. In contrast, we had less contact with the Jesuits who were priests, such as the school's headmaster and the priest who celebrated daily Mass.

Did you ever want to be a diocesan priest?

I always wanted to be a Jesuit and never considered the diocesan priesthood. I think this was because during my youth I had a lot of contact with Jesuits who were not priests, either because they were Jesuit brothers or Jesuits in formation on work experience at the school. I understood right from the start that a vocation in the Society was different from one in the diocesan priesthood. The Society was not a steppingstone to the priesthood. On the contrary, priesthood has a specific meaning within the congregation. It is considered one of the dimensions of the Apostolic religious life of the Jesuits.

How would you describe your devotion to Our Lady?

The sense of religiosity I acquired in my family, above all from my mother and my grandmothers, is directly connected to Our Lady. Every May, my mother would set up an altar to Our Lady at home, and we would place fresh flowers there daily. My paternal grandmother, Graciela, also had a huge devotion to Our Lady, in particular to Our Lady of Coromoto, who in the 1950s was declared the patroness of Venezuela. Graciela would bring images with her of Our Lady of Coromoto wherever she went. I remember going with her to Guanare, the place where the apparition had occurred. I also recall how she and a group of her friends would collect used clothing throughout the year, which they washed and mended. Then, during the fiestas for Our Lady, they would give the clothing to the poor. They called it Our Lady of Coromoto's wardrobe. Devotion to her was always linked to doing something for others. Joining the Marian Congregation, which later became known as the Community of Christian Life (CLC) was also important to me. There I learnt to pray with the Bible, to value the Eucharist, and to deepen my devotion to Our Lady.

Do you have an attachment to any particular Marian devotion?

I have a strong attachment to several. As well as to Our Lady of Coromoto, for obvious reasons and because Venezuela is always in my heart, I also have a devotion to Our Lady of Guadalupe. My parents married on her feast day, December 12, and that's the date I was baptised too. As a Jesuit I had the immense good fortune of being allowed to make my final vows on that date. I feel a close connection to Our Lady of Guadalupe, who is the patroness of Latin America and has such a beautiful story. I also have a great devotion to the Immaculate Conception, the Marian devotion we had at school. When we graduated from high school, we were given a prayer card with her image as a parting gift. Some of my contemporaries still carry it with them everywhere. Since being in Rome, I have also begun to pray for the intercession of Our Lady of La Estrada, a devotion closely linked to Ignatius and the first Jesuits.

Has there been any particularly dramatic incident in your life, akin to the wound of St. Ignatius in Pamplona, which sparked your conversion?

Rather than specific incidents, there have been many different moments. I've been shaped by a lot of different things, akin to gentle nudges that, through various experiences that opened my eyes to reality, gradually altered my outlook. Going to the hospital and the poor areas of Caracas while I was at school, for instance, shook me up, as did travelling through Venezuela with my father and also with a Jesuit brother from my school, who loved history and who every year led a group of us on a tour inland in Venezuela. Later on, other experiences were important, including taking part in the Marian Congregation in high school and coming into greater contact with the Bible, the Eucharist, and prayer. These little jolts gradually formed me. If asked to pick out one special event, however, I'd pick the thirty-day retreat of the Spiritual Exercises, which I took in the novitiate when I was 18 years old. They are the fundamental experience of the Jesuit novitiate. It was then that I realised that this was my future path.

How would you describe your personal experience of the person of Jesus at the time?

Ever since I was a small boy at the Colegio San Ignacio in Caracas, I had belonged to various groups through which I grew to know Jesus. One was the Eucharistic Crusade, where we basically read the Gospels and reflected on them. Later, as a member of the Marian Congregation during the five years I was in high school, we had a weekly meeting in which we reflected through prayer on a Bible passage, normally from the Gospels. Of that time, what I most remember is experiencing the Father, through Jesus, as the source of merciful love. I was greatly struck by the fact that the phrase "the fear of God" was much used at the time. But I did not fear God. Quite the contrary. I was not afraid of my father or my elders, and therefore feared God even less. When I entered the Society, my experience of Jesus acquired greater focus. I mentioned earlier how I found the Spiritual Exercises taken in the novitiate a truly lovely experience of Jesus. This was reinforced during my formation and has flourished throughout my life since then.

Does the person of Jesus continue to surprise you?

After being in the Society for fifty-four years, I find there is always something new in my relationship with Jesus. It never ends. It is just like what happens with human beings, whom we will never know fully because we are all continually changing. I'm always finding new riches in Jesus and never tire of returning time and again to his presence, to images of Jesus, to how he behaves in the Gospels, to encountering his presence in history. It is a beautiful relationship that impels you to grow, because with him you cannot be anyone other than your true self. You know yourself, but you are known even more fully by Jesus. It is a completely transparent relationship. For me personally, one of the loveliest experiences of all is meeting Jesus through prayer inspired by the Gospels. As one grows older, prayer becomes increasingly contemplative.

I'm always finding new riches in Jesus and never tire of returning time and again to his presence.

What was prayer like for you at the beginning, when you had just entered religious life?

Perhaps at the time it was a little more considered, because I was trying to understand a lot of new things. When I was a young man, I didn't really feel that a contemplative vocation was for me, but as time went by, I began to develop a taste for it. To quote Jeronimo Nadal, St. Ignatius says the ideal is to become a contemplative in action. To do this, one needs to develop the ability to find God in all things, which involves learning to be very attuned to contemplation. Contemplation is easier if we observe nature, but Ignatius, in fact, was referring more to the world of people, e.g., to contemplating the face of God in the poor. That is where that rich interplay of presence and absence comes into focus, when it seems as though the divine is in hiding. It is just at that moment that our founder suggests that we contemplate the Cross. There are many situations in life where it's really hard for us to see God, for example, when a child dies from a curable illness or of hunger. However, experiencing Jesus leads you to find God in all things.

How would you introduce Jesus to someone who has never heard of him?

I'd say that he is a brother, a merciful companion, the bridge between us and the Father. In the Gospels, Jesus is always taking care of others. He does so in different situations, whether he's explaining the Word of God patiently to his disciples or through signs or miracles that change someone's life. Jesus's way of living out welcome, friendship, and fraternity is moving. And we Jesuits, who call ourselves the companions of Jesus, want to emulate him. When Jesus chose his companions, the apostles, he did so, first of all, so that they could spend time with him and, later, so he could send them out as missionaries. This feeling of fellowship and fraternal community are part of what the Lord offers as the path towards the Kingdom of God.

Let's go back to your vocation. How did your family take the news that you wanted to become a Jesuit?

I imagine that my father had plans for me, but luckily he never told me about them so I never felt that I had to comply with some prescripted role. He always supported me and said that if I was sure then to go ahead and take my vocation seriously. My mother also supported me. In fact, she was very happy about it. She liked having a son who was a religious.

And did you ever fall for a girl, head over heels, at this time?

Of course, I did. In that sense, my emotional life was quite normal. I've had some very deep and serious friendships. Perhaps I never fell too deeply in love: if I had done, I would not be here today. Certainly, friendship, and especially female friendship, has been a fundamental part of my life. I have had and still have good female friends, in whom I trust deeply. I was always clear about my direction in life and fortunately, being close friends, they accepted that. Equally, each of my female friends found their own path in life and we have maintained a healthy, positive connection.

What did you want to study at university?

When I was a novice, I'd have liked to study sociology, but of course they didn't let me do that, so I followed the normal course of study for the Jesuits. I studied philosophy and then I went through regency.[3] This was in the years after the Second Vatican Council, which had a huge impact on the life of the

---

3   In Jesuit jargon, "regency" is a period of two or three years after novitiate and college studies during which the young Jesuit teaches in a Jesuit school, before going to study theology for ordination.

Church, on my school, San Ignacio in Caracas, and on my own life. In fact, the only reading matter I brought into the novitiate were the documents of the Second Vatican Council, a present from a female friend, who had been given them by her aunt in Spain, where they'd just been published by the BAC (the Spanish publisher *Biblioteca de Autores Cristianos*). At school, we were on tenterhooks during the evolution of the Council. It was clear that the Council was opening up a new era for the Church and for the Society of Jesus. Arrupe thought so too.

My generation was the first to study Philosophy in Venezuela; we did this at Andrés Bello Catholic University, which belongs to the Society. It was 1968, and both society and the Church were in a state of turmoil. In the state university, a lot was going on, and we didn't want to be left behind. We wanted to change the university statutes and, because they ignored us, we seized the Philosophy faculty. As a result, the university authorities removed us, and then threw out those they identified as the ringleaders for a while, including me.

Were you the odd one out among the Jesuits in this? Or were any others involved?

In total, five or six Jesuit philosophy students were involved. Our formators also thought like us, although there was some division within the province. Some Jesuits with more conservative ideas were quite engaged in the foundation of the Partido Social Cristiano (The Christian Social Party). We saw that path as obsolete and favoured a more populist social vision, which we'd call centre left today. They were interesting times.

After concluding your philosophy studies and a period at the Gumilla Centre, which is devoted to social outreach in Venezuela, you were sent to Rome to study Theology. How did you handle the change?

Initially, I didn't want to go because at that time for my generation it was hugely important to study in Latin America, where the Latin American version of Liberation Theology was really kicking off. A movement was emerging to explore the kind of faith experienced in pastoral care for the people. At that time in El Salvador, Ellacuria and his group had just begun their work, and we were determined to join them. And also go to Chile, then under the government of Salvador Allende, where a theological-political phenomenon was emerging. But the murder of Rutilio Grande put an end to any thoughts the provincial of the Society had of sending me to El Salvador. Ultimately, it was Arrupe who decided I should go to Rome, because he had just founded the International College at the Gesù and wanted students from all over the world to go there. I saw this as a step backwards, theologically speaking, because at the time we thought that the Gregorian University was in the dark ages, although I discovered we were wrong about that. It was a magnificent centre of learning, with really good teachers, above all in the whole field of biblical studies. The style of teaching was perhaps a tad formal, but the formation on offer was very solid.

You were ordained a priest after returning to Venezuela to study for your fourth year of Theology. Who ordained you?

The then-Bishop of San Cristóbal, Alejandro Fernández Feo, who had also baptised me. He was a good family friend, so much so that we used to called him "Father Uncle" because as a young man he had been the parish priest in Antímano en Caracas, where my paternal grandparents lived. He took part in the Council, which he had some reservations about, and it was hard for him to accept that both I and one of my cousins had become Jesuits rather than diocesan priests. He ordained me in Barquisimeto, halfway between Caracas and Maracaibo, where the companion with whom I was ordained had worked. For my first Mass I chose the Bible passage about the grain of wheat which will not produce fruit unless it dies. I wanted to explain that I was becoming a Jesuit in order to serve other people, because I thought of the religious life and the priesthood as an apostolic service via which you give your life.

Afterwards you studied political sciences. How would you describe the experience?

This was at the state university, the Central University of Venezuela, whose lecture halls were in the throes of the prevailing zeitgeist. For at least two years, I studied Marx's *Das Kapital*. Just as I had studied the Gospels and the whole Bible during my theological studies, so I had to do the same thing with *Das Kapital* and other classic Communist and Socialist texts. This coincided with a time when there was great criticism of Soviet Communism, and a vision of non-Soviet socialism was beginning to emerge, not least in Venezuela.

Did you ever get the chance to discover first-hand what life was really like in a Soviet country?

I went a few times to Cuba, which could not have been any more Soviet, and it made an enormous impression on me: the food rationing, the state of the cities... It was awful. And this was in a time of some economic growth. These years were very intense and also defined by the great frustration of what had happened with the Sandinista revolution in Nicaragua. We followed all these processes from the Gumilla Centre in Caracas, where I worked on research, studied, and did some university teaching. At the same time, we published the monthly SIC magazine and offered social-political formation to base ecclesial communities.

In the light of the huge commitment you have to your country, when you see the state Venezuela is in now, how do you feel?

I weep. Just weep. More out of pain than anger. Everything that has happened is really hard to take, as is the story of my own family. My father was the first professional in the family. One of my grandparents was an emigrant who left Spain due to poverty. My experience was of a Venezuela that was growing and expanding in every sense of the word: socially, economically, democratically, and politically. It had flaws, which were exactly what we were criticising, but this critique was intended to be constructive, part of a process. I never dreamt that so much could be destroyed. The country began to founder from around 2002 onwards, when there was a general strike during which Hugo Chávez, then president since 1992, was ousted from the government for three days. There had been symptoms of the problems before this, but that was the moment when everything that Nicolas Maduro would later inherit all came together in a Gordian knot of power that held the country captive.

Right from the start I thought that in terms of Venezuela's political development, Hugo Chavez was a step backwards. I did not agree with his concept of political-military power, which he would later describe as "21st-century Socialism." In an interview I gave shortly after Chavez's election, I compared him to a "democratic Caesar." This paradoxical expression was used by positivist thinkers during the Venezuelan dictatorship of the 1920s, and in my opinion, could also apply to Chavez. It involves the concept of the caudillo, the *Duce*, in whom all power is concentrated as the representative of the people. In my opinion, Chavez represented a throwback to that concept of power due to how he related to the people, the party, and army. For my generation, separating the army from politics was a question of life or death: democracy is possible only if the army and politics are kept separate.

Did you have any personal contact with Chavez?

We used to talk, before he won the elections. At the time, a Jesuit, Luis Maria Olaso, was in charge of the human rights brief at the office of the Attorney General of the Republic, and alongside Olaso I went to visit Chavez in prison after the military coup of 1992. There was a public debate over what Chavez wanted to do. Our relationship was good but tempered with criticism. We argued a lot, although he said we had saved his life. In one sense that's true. After he was imprisoned, they wanted to move him and other companions to another prison and there was some fear that they were going to kill him on the way. Olaso, a bishop, and I offered to travel with him in the vehicle. The situation was very tense, but we wanted to build bridges. After he became president, we saw him a few more times. He had a concept of power that was reinforced by his contact with Fidel Castro: an

idea that power should be absolute, one sole authority with a
military branch, a civil branch, and a political branch. That is
what he set about doing and what Nicolas Maduro, whom I have
never met, has continued to implement.

*Can you foresee a way out of the conflict Venezuela is going
through?*

I would really love to do that. It will be sorted out some-
day, but I don't know when. First of all, Venezuela needs to get
through the situation it's in right now. What Chavism represents,
this way of understanding the State and the Government, needs
to radically change, and that's not going to be easy. It needs
to be defeated, and the political system and economy need to
be rebuilt, which won't happen overnight. Free and transparent
elections could kickstart that change and prove a turning point.
The fragmentation of the opposition is a significant obstacle to
that happening. I don't want to downplay their merits at all, as
they include people who have risked their lives and have done
a lot of the right things, but they have also made mistakes and
a unified strategy has been lacking. There have been missed
opportunities.

*In the light of the strong bond you have always felt with your
country, have you ever felt a call to go as a missionary to another
country or thought of staying in Venezuela to help with its
development?*

I felt a vocation to be a missionary to my country, where we
had much to contribute because the province was very young,
the Church was very fragile, and the nation was going through

a very interesting time. If I'd been sent elsewhere, I'd have accepted this happily, but I didn't feel that particular call.

You were the first Venezuelan to be elected Provincial of Venezuela in 1996, and later you were named Rector of the Catholic University of Táchira, in San Cristóbal. How did you end up in that role?

The Bishop of San Cristóbal, who baptised me and ordained me a priest, had the foresight to create a university in this region on the edge of Venezuela, 1,200 kilometres from Caracas, and he asked the Jesuits to manage it. That was how, after eight years being Provincial, I ended up as Rector. I felt at home in the university world, but I had never previously held a role in it. It was a relatively small university, although when I left, we had 8,000 students and had to build a new campus. It is on the border with Colombia, which is why we created various cross-border initiatives as part of a network with other institutions.

You were the youngest Jesuit to take part in the 33rd General Congregation held in 1983, where Peter-Hans Kolvenbach was elected the Superior General. What was that like?

Really lovely. I took the opportunity visit Father Arrupe in the infirmary nearly every day. Due to his poor health, we could communicate only through looks and gestures. A beautiful experience. I'd met Arrupe when he made a trip to Venezuela, and afterwards he continued to be very much part of our lives through his letters and his activities as Superior General. The session where Father Arrupe was in the hall of the Congregation and offered his resignation was quite moving.

The election of the new Superior General, Peter-Hans Kolvenbach, was just unforgettable. In the midst of a very tense time in the Church, the companion capable of leading the Society was elected: the fruit of a consensus only possible through the Holy Spirit. It was also important for me to encounter the universality of the Society, embodied by the huge diversity of individuals, cultures, points of views, who gather during this kind of assembly.

You also took part in the General Congregation 35 in 2008, where Adolfo Nicolas was elected as Superior General and, finally, the General Congregation 36 in 2016, where you yourself were elected. Did you have any idea you were in the running? Did you know there were bets on you being elected?

I never dreamt I would be elected. At the time I was in charge of the Society's international houses in Rome, and the possibility didn't even enter my mind. I knew that I'd been a candidate for some post in Rome linked to social justice. But at the end, I was to take a different road.

When Nicolas asked you to move to Rome to take charge of the Society's international houses, did that appeal to you?

No, to tell you the truth, but as at other times of my life, I accepted it because it was the will of God, something quite beyond my control. That is what I entered the Society for: to accept the plans my brothers had for me and to give myself to those plans with all my mind, heart, body, and soul. I am not nostalgic about the places, plans, and projects I have left behind.

Is working in the office that belonged before you to Arrupe,
Kolvenbach, and Nicolas a heavy responsibility?

Yes, it is. Can you imagine how I felt when I entered the office
and thought, "This is where Fr. Pedro Arrupe lived"? But I had
known Fr. Kolvenbach better. We worked together a great deal
and it was he who taught me about governance. I learnt a lot from
his style of leadership as the Jesuit Superior. He knew how to give
you a great deal of freedom without pressuring you, how to trust
you yet be clear when the time had come to say what he thought.
I also had a strong relationship with Fr. Nicolas and learnt much
from him too, especially from his humane style of governance.

How have you coped with the various roles and responsibilities
that the Society has entrusted to you?

I've let myself go with the flow, through a radical trust in
God, who is present in each of the companions with whom I
work here in the General Curia. Each one has his own particular
experience and formation. We had not worked together previously. Nicolas, by the end of his term of General, used to say,
"We, the General," which is a way of saying that the General is
nobody without his team. That's something I totally subscribe
to. St. Ignatius used to say that the secretary of the Society was
the hands, eyes, and memory of the General.

You lead one of the largest male congregations in the Catholic
Church and your decisions have consequences for the lives of
many people. How do you understand the exercise of power? Did
you sleep better before becoming the General?

I still don't have any problems sleeping. Rather than a feeling
of power, I have a feeling of responsibility, of being obliged to

take decisions, which arise after a process of discernment rather than according to the first idea that comes into my head or what might seem a good idea to me personally. There needs to be a process that involves discernment. This isn't something private, and it demands an effort. I try to do things as well as I possibly can, devoting all my physical and spiritual energy to the task at hand.

I'm struck by a phrase attributed to John Paul II. Whenever he analysed a complex issue with his team or wasn't sure what decision to take, he would say to them that they had not prayed enough. Francis also uses that expression occasionally. Does it apply to you?

I completely agree with it. That's the style of governance we want. We should test the questions we ponder in the purifying fire of prayer. It isn't enough to just study or discuss them. I think that this is one of the things we have learnt to do in an explicit fashion. In the process that led to the formulation of the Universal Apostolic Preferences, we wanted to do things this way, and I believe we succeeded. A deep deliberation was held, with as much space given to personal and community prayer as to group discernment.

> **We should test the questions we ponder in the purifying fire of prayer.**

At the present time, it seems we struggle to say "no." Is that true for you?

Of course, it is a struggle, but it is necessary. In my years of experience of governance, I can see that saying no does a great deal of good. The "no's" I've received and those I've had to give have done good, both to me and to others. This is important in every field and, of course, in governance too. Sometimes it's hard to say "no" because you are really excited about a given project or group. It's hard, but it does good, in emotional issues too.

What do you feel when you think about death?

I'm afraid of dying in pain, through torture, or with unmerited suffering. But I don't think very much about death. It's not something that comes to mind often. I have been much struck by a phrase in the Gospel that says that we have already passed from death to life, and that whole concept of being saved and participating through grace in the life of God. Death is the end of a stage, a transition that is not always easy. This is true of the martyrs or of people who spend a long time in this transition period due to long drawn-out illness.

TIMES, PEOPLES, AND PLACES

A red thread runs through many of the paintings of the Bosnian artist Safet Zec. This detail can be clearly observed in his work, *Deposition from the Cross*[4], which is kept in the chapel that holds the remains of Fr. Arrupe in the Church of the Gesù in Rome. The thread, sometimes resembling a blood stain, is discreet, weaving together different times in history, people, and places, to reveal in a unique and continuous narrative the profound unity of the human race. This is the blood we share, offering a sense of human familiarity that opens up paths to fraternity and hope.

Our individual stories also interweave with the stories of others, as well as with the specific events and places that have revealed our gifts and our limitations—and wrought from us our successes and failures. The story weaving together the places, spaces, and times in our lives anchors the roots of our identity. Every process of conversion has a story behind it whose humus the Lord has gradually opened to bring forth new life, a life in abundance (Jn 10:10). Conversion does not deny the past, but it does transform it into compost that fertilises our witness of what is possible for the person who trusts in divine grace. Conversion is not a one-off, isolated life experience. It is a process filled with encounters with God, with ourselves, and with others.

---

4 Safet Sec, *Deposition from the Cross*, Church of the Gesù, Rome, 2014.

PRAYER POINTS

Composition of place. Recall some of the places that have had personal significance for you.

Grace to ask for. Lord, allow me to recognise you at work in the people, events, and places of my life.

First point. Remember those people who have shaped your life and who have helped you "seek and find" the will of God. Give thanks for them and draw spiritual profit from this.

Second point. Recall the times when God has been generous in revealing himself to you and has helped aspects of your life to grow. Give thanks and draw spiritual profit from this.

BIBLE TEXT

Acts 22:3–23: The Conversion of St. Paul

» Can you identify a particular time when you started to see your own life and that of those around you with God's eyes? What was this like?

» Who has helped you grow in human terms and as a believer? How did they do this?

» Where is the Lord inviting you to grow in your life today?

Colloquy. As though you were chatting with a friend, tell Jesus how you have been noticing his presence in your life. Let him tell you how he has been making himself present in your story. Finish with an Our Father and a Hail Mary. Do not forget to examine what you have experienced during this prayer time.

TIPS FOR SPIRITUAL CONVERSATION

For spiritual conversation starting with personal prayer, the following steps from the general methodology of spiritual conversation are recommended (p. 268).

For spiritual conversation concerning an apostolic work, the following prayer points may be beneficial:

Composition of place. Remember with thanks the individuals, projects and apostolic dreams which have shaped the story of the work.

Grace to ask for. Lord, help me to acknowledge the foundations—the people, events and projects—of this apostolic work.

Bible text. Matthew 7:24–27. Which parts of this work have become the bedrock supporting the mission and our teamwork? Which parts turn the foundations into sand? What is the Lord calling us to?

Colloquy. As though you were chatting with a friend, tell Jesus about the dreams and hopes you have for this mission and allow him to tell you how he envisions this apostolate. Finish with an Our Father and a Hail Mary. Don't forget to examine what you have experienced during this prayer time. The fruits of this time may be shared, in accordance with the steps of general methodology for Spiritual Conversation.

The pandemic has been difficult for everyone: it has changed the life of some and led others to face death. It has revealed serious problems but has also helped us see with fresh eyes, making the need for a radical change to our world order more obvious, plus the fact that every Christian needs to play a role in this transformation.

3 Bold Living in Today's World

Easter. Peter Girasek, SJ

Has COVID-19 generated a new crisis or just made worse the problems the world already suffered from?

No matter how much we repeat this, we still can't quite believe that we are facing a change of era. The pandemic has revealed the cracks in the system, the fragility of the structures of a world that is ending while another is born. It has brought to light structural injustice, a phenomenon we have denounced for the past forty years and which is now spreading from one era to the next.

One of the challenges the pandemic has obviously highlighted is globalisation, without which the health crisis would probably have been less widespread. We need to review our ideas about globalisation. Is it a process to try and make us all homogenous, as the delusion of the free market would claim? Or does it respect and make the most of human diversity so that we may live in a multi-colour world?

Rather than placing us all in the same boat, the Coronavirus has compelled us to sail through the same fierce storm. We are not all in the same boat; for some people, the impact of the waves has been more apparent than for others. The great problems of the world that existed before the pandemic, are now more obvious. Hopefully, we can learn the lesson and draw conclusions that inspire us to take the decisions necessary to defeat the root cause of the problems.

And what do you see as the fundamental problems?

There are so many. I'll name a few, but also take this opportunity to recommend the Pope's encyclical, *Fratelli tutti*. In the first chapter, the Pope gives a good description of the most serious problems facing humanity. In my opinion, the greatest challenge is that humanity has not developed a shared sense of the common good, including the care of the environment. That is why I believe the political awareness of every individual, of our leaders, and our society overall, needs developing. Jesuit schools, universities, and social centres are already working on this. We're trying to provide some formation: first of all, to motivate the students in our schools and universities and those linked to our social centres to have a greater awareness of the possibility of changing the political discourse and steering our societies towards a greater sense of solidarity and respect for the dignity of every human being.

Can the common good of humanity and our planet by defined by politics?

Yes. The political domain is part of our identity as people. Individuals should not cut themselves off by focusing on their own well-being but should seek the common good of all in society. There are factors that, as the Pope says, clearly develop better politics. One would be abandoning war as an instrument of power. Another is rejecting societal violence, which comes in many forms, quite apart from the ideologies that promote or justify this. Politics must become a space for another way of distributing goods, so that poverty and the scandal of inequality, which has not diminished despite economic growth, may be overcome. This is one of the biggest core problems. Then there is the challenge posed by the digital universe. Science and technology can prove overwhelming and invade every area of our lives. We should guarantee every people the ability to conserve their culture, but also their access to knowledge and information, albeit through tools that are truly at the service of wisdom and truth.

Do you believe that there is also a crisis of ethics and values today?

That idea makes me uneasy because it deifies the past by suggesting that once upon a time our society and political leaders were guided by values and ethics. I don't view the current crisis as an exceptional period but as a tension within the individual and in history in the quest for meaning. We all have to find that meaning, as individuals and as a people. In this change of epoch, the need is particularly acute.

How long do you think this time of transition between the new epoch you foresee and the one we are leaving behind will last?

That's very hard to predict. It might last for more than a generation. The durability of the world that is coming into being remains to be seen. It's possible the process is now accelerating compared to that of previous ages, but I wouldn't dare to make predictions. One of the hallmarks of our highly inter-connected world is that it never stands still. Humanity is changing more now than in the past. Knowledge emerges more quickly and circulates more efficiently now.

While analysing this change of epoch, it is worth recalling Pope Francis's prophetic insistence on opening up new processes rather than occupying spaces, i.e., highlighting the importance of venturing to open up new paths and travel along them, rather than settle down into securities that paralyse us. This involves being willing to follow this change in epoch, to allow ourselves to be swept along in the hands of God on a path we are learning about as we go down it. It's a bit nerve-wracking, but that's completely normal when you grapple with transcendence. We need to live boldly: it is hair-raising but yields great satisfaction.

The pandemic has revealed that the securities upon which many people based their lives were false. How can this void be filled now? Have you in any way re-connected with your own fragility?

Long before the pandemic, I was aware of my own fragility. I have never felt strong. Before I was two years old, I developed an illness that clogged my bronchial tubes and left me suffering from allergic asthma for years. While I was a child, this recurred every so often. Two of my sisters also had allergic asthma, and my mother had many sleepless nights taking care of us. When unable to breathe, an asthmatic is assailed with feelings of great discomfort, which brings them face to face with their vulnerability. I remember that as a child, I sometimes found myself being unable to breathe while I was running en route to the mountains, or in the middle of the night. I would then rely on a bronchodilator to breathe freely. I underwent treatment for years, and eventually I was free from my asthma, but that feeling of vulnerability has never left me.

I have also been fragile intellectually and spiritually. I've never felt that I was the best-formed Jesuit nor the most solid spiritually. I feel my fragility constantly, and this pushes me to place myself wholly in God's hands. For many people, the pandemic has been an invitation to reflect on what they based their sense of security on, and to look at why they had once felt invincible. The starting point of the Spiritual Exercises is exploring where and in what we have placed our trust, and what the foundation of our identity is based upon. The Exercises are a path to placing your trust in something outside yourself: God made manifest through Jesus. Therefore, this feeling that we're fragile is very welcome.

Could a world that is better than the one we had beforehand come out of the Coronavirus?

It's possible but I don't think anyone can guarantee that will be the outcome. The obstacles preventing that are, in addition, pretty substantial. A change in attitude was evident, for instance, between the first and second wave of the pandemic. At first, at least in Italy, the crisis was seen as an opportunity for things to change. After the recurrence of the virus, that vanished. What prevailed instead was weariness and a feeling of discouragement in the light of the restrictions, plus a desire to return to what was previously thought of as normality.

To achieve real change, we need to be bold, which is a far from normal attitude, since it entails abandoning our comfort zone: what we once had, what we have known and has been familiar. Courage is needed to face an unknown path, which can include risks that we are not always willing to take. Mary of Nazareth possessed this boldness when facing the impossible. Jesus was also bold. In fact, it could be said he was mad, in the light of what he suggested in the Beatitudes. This boldness is not within everyone's reach, but there are people, stirred by love, who enthuse others with their struggle for solidarity and become the yeast in the dough. The challenge is that there is an enormous amount of dough. And it is in no way easy

> **To achieve real change, we need to be bold.**

to ferment, to allow the kind of radical transformation that leads to a better world.

Has the pandemic obliged the Society of Jesus to change its direction?

It's changed our modus operandi, because circumstances have changed radically, albeit with many local variations. But our direction has not changed. It has rather been fully confirmed since it was set by the Second Vatican Council, which shaped our path of working for reconciliation and faith coupled with justice. Additionally, we have the Universal Apostolic Preferences, which give us four cardinal points, and also the initiative, established before the pandemic, of making the Ignatian Year a time to promote processes of conversion. Everything we have gone through with the Coronavirus, including the increasing fragility of our apostolic works and their financial basis, is equipping us to continue on our course, only in greater depth.

How has the pandemic affected the Society?

In every conceivable way. Many of our communities had cases of the virus. More than 100 Jesuits died of the Coronavirus in 2020. That hasn't been the only impact. It's also sparked uncertainty about whether we can carry on with what we were doing before. This has been particularly apparent in our educational institutions where the impact of the crisis has been significant. Let's not forget, however, that the pandemic has also unleashed tremendous energy and revealed an astonishing resilience in many people. A good example of this comes from the British Province, where we have a small spirituality centre in Glasgow. When they began to offer online programs, there was a huge increase in the numbers taking part. No one sat down to cry over spilt milk. Instead, we focused on looking at how we might respond to what we were going through with the resources at our disposal. Our schools, for instance, threw themselves into long-distance teaching. And in places where technological resources were scarce, classes were given via the radio, or the teachers made house visits to hand out and later collect homework. There was also an enormous outpouring of creativity to respond to the most immediate needs, such as finding food and medicine. The challenge is not returning to how things were before the crisis but how to make a long-term change. We know the path to take.

How do you think that the Coronavirus might affect capitalism?

There are various ways to understand capitalism. It's a system that has demonstrated an enormous capacity to adapt to new circumstances. What we know as capitalism today has little in common with the ideas it began with. The pandemic confirmed its adaptability, not only in the sectors of business that thrived, e.g., those connected to technology, communication, or healthcare. It also led to reflection on the role of the State, one of the core ideas in capitalist thinking. Today, few people would dare to suggest that the State should be reduced to a minimum or demand that there should be no regulation on freedom or defend privatisation as the answer to problems of economic development. After the attack on the Twin Towers in New York in 2001, unfettered freedom as a concept was relinquished. Now, we accept that freedom has to have limits for reasons of health or safety.

The challenge we face as a society is how to transform capitalism in order to attain another, participatory and truly democratic social structure that is inclusive, and in which the common good, access for all to goods and services, and protecting the environment, are paramount.

How will the pandemic change the Church? Has it accelerated secularisation?

The Church's remit is not opposed to secular society, although that is what some sectors of the Church would like. We should open our doors and find ways to dialogue with the secular world. I believe that, more than a spike in religiosity, what is happening with the pandemic is that our experience of God is going deeper. Out of that, the meaning of community and communion could undergo a revival. We're moving away from a vision of the Church that could be called clerical, in which the visibility of churches or symbols like priests are paramount, towards one in which various forms of lived experience prevail. This should lead to a lessening of clericalism, which is an attempt to control and manipulate religion. This is where the pandemic is having a positive effect because it's making us ask questions that many of us were not asking before it.

Do you think it a tragedy that in many places the Churches were closed during lockdown?

Those who complained about this complained beforehand that in some places, the churches were half empty. One of the most significant outcomes of this period is the need to leave church buildings. Having to shut the churches for health reasons is obliging us to think through our relationship with the community in other ways. There are many ways of experiencing the sacraments. Those who mourn the closure of parishes have perhaps never had personal experience of places where the Church barely has any buildings and faith is lived out in other ways. To give a few examples, in the Amazon region, parts of Russia, and parts of the Democratic Republic of the Congo, there are villages where priests are frequently not seen for months during much of the year, but where, even so, there is an astonishing fidelity to the life and mission of the community. The Spirit of God is at work everywhere. The Church does the best she can to provide spaces and places where the Spirit can express itself, but the Spirit is not limited to those places and spaces. The closure of Churches can be seen as a wake-up call from the Holy Spirit so that the community may depend less on the Church being in a building and learn how to live out the faith creatively in other circumstances.

The 19th and 20th centuries were shaped by ideological struggles. Which ideologies today could prove to be a trap?

All ideology is deceptive because it distorts freedom of thought. Ideology is like wearing a pair of spectacles that oblige you to see things only one way. That is quite different to ideas, which I hope everyone has, to help them make sense of the world. Ideology, in contrast, presents one, unique, unchanging point of view, which limits freedom of thought. Its reach can extend beyond the organisation of a given society or economy and define every aspect of someone's life. Some people live as though communism or socialism were their religion, but religion may also be experienced as if it were an ideology. Fundamentalism can sometimes be the outcome of exposure to an ideology or some religions.

Ignatian spirituality is radically anti-ideological because its guiding principles are interior freedom, discernment, and choosing between different options at particular times, in specific situations. What is recommended first of all in the *Spiritual Exercises* is a quest that arises only when you are unsure which direction to take. Later on, there's an examen to evaluate the path taken. If you take Ignatian spirituality seriously, you have a good antidote to ideology. That's even more the case when it is reinforced by the formation and intellectual curiosity that a Jesuit education attempts to foster.

> **If you take Ignatian spirituality seriously, you have a good antidote to ideology.**

Are there any members of the Society of Jesus today who may have been "contaminated" by ideology?

It is possible because all of us are subject to ideological temptations. There are times when, for psychological or circumstantial reasons, you need to feel grounded and cling to something clear and safe that allows you to interpret what is going on in the world. No vaccine is 100 per cent proof against that. The only cure is to hold on to a living experience of God, who is with us on our journey even when it may not feel very stable. This involves real listening to God's voice in humanity and the world and being attentive to the signs of the times. Our example is Abraham: like him, we can set out on our journey even if we're unsure where it will lead us.

How can we respond to the "Third World War being fought piecemeal," which the Pope says has been waging in the world for some years now?

This topic is connected to the idea of politics I set out earlier. We can respond by strengthening a sense of universal citizenship so that it upholds structures that respond to the common good in the long term. However, this approach won't really be feasible if we don't first develop our sense of the universal and political. The Arrupe Centre in Palermo and the San Fedele Centre in Milan are really trying to help people develop this political awareness as individuals and then go a step beyond this by helping the society around them. If we are to have a real awareness of this "piecemeal World War III" and come up with policies that counter it, we need to feel that we are citizens of the world.

This leads us to invest in a holistic education that forms people in the awareness that they are world citizens. It's also a wake-up call to religions so that they may avoid becoming ideologies that justify war. That also happened to Christianity at particular points in history. Religions are true to themselves only if they always promote peace and reconciliation. The best response to this "piecemeal Third World War," however, comes from education, inter-religious dialogue, and a long-term vision for humanity. Wars equal the absence of politics. They arise when peoples cannot resolve their conflicts through dialogue.

> **Religions are true to themselves only if they always promote peace and reconciliation.**

*In his encyclical Fratelli Tutti, and other documents and state-
ments, the Pope returns time and again to the concept of the
people. What role can popular movements play today?*

Francis has salvaged the concept of the people by invest-
ing the term with a very deep ecclesial and political meaning.
We become individuals when we become part of a people and
step outside ourselves to be part of a community that seeks justice, peace, and the well-being of all. Chapter V of *Fratelli Tutti*
offers a valuable reflection on a better kind of politics, starting
with the category of the people. The Second Vatican Council
defines the Church as the People of God, which means that we
all belong to the same people. Francis resorts frequently to this
concept, which has a longstanding Biblical and Christian tradition: it is no coincidence he is expressing himself in these terms.

When it comes to popular movements, we enter into political categories. Francis is reclaiming the concept of the people
as political protagonists and, in this context, he appreciates the
value of popular movements, of citizens who organise themselves in order to fight for their rights. There is a risk, we should
not forget, that the people may be manipulated by ideologies, by
parties, or authoritarian figures.

*Populism also exists. Do you fear that the pandemic may increase
the success of populist movements and parties, some of which use
religion in an opportunistic fashion?*

Populisms strip the concept of the people of meaning. They
act as a substitute for the people and subjugate them. Populisms
do not take the people seriously, as the Pope warns in *Fratelli
Tutti*. Whoever takes the people seriously will not slide into

populism. Something similar occurs with clericalism, which does not take the laity in the Church seriously. This is a form of ecclesial populism in which the clergy replace the Christian people. That risk is always present, which is why we need to be very clear about the concept of the people and the experience of becoming the people.

And we should not forget authoritarianism, which is a constant temptation in every domain: in the family, sports groups, religious communities, or society in general. It is constantly lurking in political, financial, and religious circles. Power can drift towards authoritarianism. The change of era and the pandemic have generated a sense of uncertainty in many people, and as a survival mechanism, they are trying to latch on to an idea or an individual.

Can a Christian be true to their faith if they are not concerned about immigrants?

Allow me to relay an autobiographical anecdote here. I am the grandson of a migrant originally from Liérganes, a town in Santander in northern Spain who arrived in Venezuela at age eighteen at the start of the 20th century. He became totally integrated into his host nation to the extent that in the 1940s, when the process of issuing identity cards began in Venezuela and his friends wanted to give him one, he refused to accept it. He said he did not need it because he had been in the country for decades, and this was where he had his wife, his children, his house, and his money. And that when he died, his remains would stay there, as happened in due course. Thanks to his decision, today I am able to have a Spanish passport as well as a Venezuelan one and a Vatican one. Obviously, I am not an emigrant in the same way that my grandfather was, but I can move around Europe just like any European, thanks to the fact that he emigrated. I mention this because it strikes me that Europe and the United States have forgotten their origins, the memory of being emigrants. Every people is the result of emigration. That memory, which my grandfather retained faithfully and passed on to us, was essential. The Bible invites us to recall the story of the migrant People of God, which is why we should welcome the stranger wherever we meet them. When we maintain this memory, we're able to welcome and integrate other people. The great challenge facing Europe and the United States is to feel that being a migrant is inherent to their identity.

A change in the political, social, and financial domain will be impossible to achieve without committed leaders. How can we get leaders with sufficiently different mindsets to build a better world?

Leaders do not spring up by chance. They are formed in families, communities, and reference groups. This is an issue linked to the question of politics mentioned earlier. The first step towards having leaders with a broad mindset comes from formation in politics and citizenship. The Society of Jesus includes this element in all its apostolates. One of our greatest current responsibilities is political formation so that everyone may develop a sense of citizenship. This is greatly needed.

We need to do more to form people who are called to public service and who can draw on an experience of Ignatian spirituality. This includes insights that can help with decision making and intellectual formation so that public service may be understood to mean the search for the common good and plans for its implementation.

Is forming leaders one of the main challenges today for the world and the Church?

Yes. We're seeing so many examples of failure of leadership in politics. We've also seen examples in the Church of leaders failing to take appropriate action in regard to accusations of sexual abuse. Pope Francis is highlighting a synodal model of leadership for the Church, which entails greater participation and discernment, respecting the fact that the Holy Spirit is at work at much within every individual as in the community. We have started a program to develop synodal and discernment leadership. It is a project in partnership with the umbrella groups of male and female religious orders and congregations (the International Union of Female Superiors General—UISG and the Union of Male Superiors General—USG). It is backed by the Gregorian University and involves teachers from some of the principal Jesuit business administration schools. The hope is that, in a humble way, we may be able to offer Vatican bureaucrats, male and female religious superiors, and lay people with responsibilities within the Church, the opportunity to think together, to dream together, and to acquire the skills required to move that dream forward.

Are you in favour of political parties that present themselves as Christian?

One cannot be fully Christian if one does not actively participate in politics. This can be done in many ways, and through more than one party, in the awareness that political parties are not the only form of political participation. The search for the common good should be present in all political strains, but it is a plus that today there are scarcely any parties left that call themselves Catholic or Christian. It is good that the Church is not associated with a particular ideology or a unique political program. We should concern ourselves with forming people to take part in public life, which they can do in different parties, all of which should be united by an awareness of the common good. Despite the negative reaction that the word *party* evokes, when they do not exist at all, it is a sign of weak democracy.

Jesuit universities exist for many reasons, including to encourage and develop critical thinking. We want our professors and students to be equipped to unmask ideologies and false ways of thinking that undermine the individual and society. In the last century, we witnessed political ideologies including Nazism, Stalinism, Communism, and Fascism. Consumerism, capitalism, and socialism were also imbued with ideological overtones. As was also the case with clericalism, a mindset profoundly entrenched in many of our practices in the Church. All these ideologies undermine the solidarity and dignity of the human person. Jesuit universities and Catholic universities in general can play a role in denouncing such ideologies and helping people to protect themselves against them.

"SEEING VARIOUS PEOPLE" [SE 106]

One of the most attractive paintings at the Museo del Prado in Madrid is *The Garden of Earthly Delights* (c. 1490–1500) a triptych by Jheronimus van Aken, also known as Hieronymus Bosch.[5] An enigmatic work, filled with many subtleties and details, it represents the road from Heaven to Hell. The common thread linking together each panel is sin. In the central panel appear many, quite diverse people, all captive to sinful pleasures and destined for a Hell littered with musical instruments intended to torture all who end up there. Ultimately, this represents the failure of the human race, irredeemably heading towards eternal condemnation. It is a work replete with an intriguing variety of colours, figures, and scenes, but at heart what it illustrates is the scale of the failure of God's plan for his creation.

St. Ignatius, in his contemplation of the Incarnation [SE 101–109] invites us to contemplate how the Trinity regards the world in all its diversity: how some people live in peace while others are at war, how some weep and others laugh, how some people are healthy and others ill, and while some are born, others die. The Trinity looks at the reality of the world just as it is. However, it does not resign itself to imminent failure or with the passivity of a person watching the frustration of their dreams. On the contrary, the Trinity does something unexpected and quite inconceivable: it decides that the Son should become incarnate in the centre of history, that he should become man to save the human race. "God wants all people to be saved and to come to a knowledge of the truth" (1 Timothy 2:4). That is why he keeps nothing to himself, even his own Son, in order that we might attain salvation. Faced with a distortion of his plan, God offers incarnation. In the face of

---

5 You can appreciate the work and obtain information about the artist with the following link: https://bit.ly/2Yzlcle.

what is apparently lost, he offers total self-giving. By interacting with us in this way, God encourages us to commit ourselves to walk alongside the full reality of humankind and to take a gamble on hope.

PRAYER POINTS

Preparatory prayer. Ask God our Lord for the grace that all my intentions, actions, and operations may be ordered purely to the service and praise of the Divine Majesty (*SE* 46; cf. *SE* 23).

Composition of place. To dwell on all the different situations around you or which you have been asked to accompany.

Grace to ask for. Lord, grant me the grace to know you deeply, you who for my sake engage with the different situations of this world, so that I may love and follow you even more.

First point. To truly see the people around you in their gifts and their flaws, with their realities and challenges. Reflect on this and draw spiritual benefit from this.

Second point. Consider how the Trinity sees the reality of the people around you.

Third point. Using your imagination, examine your daily reality and let the signs of God's presence emerge in its midst.

BIBLE TEXTS

Luke 1:26–38 / Titus 3:4–7 / Ephesians 3:14–21

» How would you describe the situation around you? Can you see signs of God's presence? What does this situation inspire you to do?

» Which commitments does this daily situation inspire you to accept? Given the immense variety of situations and people involved, what do you think would lead you closer to the Kingdom of God?

» How might you communicate hope, acknowledge human dignity, and the need to care for creation, etc., within this situation? Where do you find God's ongoing concern for his creation?

Colloquy. As though chatting with a friend, speak to God the Father, who has created everything out of love, for you and for the whole of humanity. Let him tell you about his plan for the world, and if you feel inspired to do so, offer with generosity to partner with him. Finish with an Our Father and a Hail Mary. Do not forget to examine what you have experienced during this prayer time.

TIPS FOR SPIRITUAL CONVERSATION

For spiritual conversation that arises from personal prayer, the following steps from the general methodology of spiritual conversation are recommended (p. 268).

For spiritual conversation concerning an apostolic work, the following prayer points may be beneficial.

Composition of place. Consider the variety of people and situations involved in the mission of Christ that you cooperate with.

Grace to ask for. Lord, help me recognise your invitations in the specific context which you ask me to accompany.

Bible text. Mark 6:34–44. What is the Lord inviting us to do in the mission he has entrusted to us and called upon us to accompany? Who is stirring up our compassion? What kind of hunger are we being called to satiate?

Colloquy. As though chatting with a friend, speak to God the Father, who has created everything through love and who cares for the whole of humanity. Allow him to tell you about his plan for this specific place where you are cooperating with his mission. Finish with an Our Father and a Hail Mary. Do not forget to examine what you have experienced during the prayer time. The fruits of this prayer may be shared, in accordance with the steps of general methodology for Spiritual Conversation.

As has always been the case during its 2,000-year history, the Church grapples with new challenges every day, responding with serenity to each one, in the light of its divine origin and terrestrial foundation. It is a Church which seeks to grow as the People of God moving forward, at the service of the most needy, living out and preaching the good news of Jesus.

4 A New Dream for the Church

The washing of the feet (detail from the triptych, The Story of the Table).
Pablo Walker, SJ

The Church is often compared to a transatlantic ocean liner, akin to a vast vessel that struggles to change direction, does so slowly, and what's more, keeps chugging along at the same pace for miles. After the volte-face of Vatican II, where is the Christian community heading?

As the Second Vatican Council reminded us, the Church is the People of God as a whole and not just the hierarchy. Personally, I really like the image of the Church as a boat, which dates from its origins, because a boat's situation is determined by its location. It might find itself in tranquil waters, with an abundance of fish or in the middle of a storm and about to capsize. Its crew members can spend the whole night toiling yet fail to catch a single fish.

There is a second, complementary image that St. Paul and St. Ignatius prefer: of the Church as a body in need of all its parts. Returning to the image of the boat, however, obviously it is complicated to steer, and to sail it in such diverse waters requires experience and a team in which different responsibilities are assigned to every individual. So where is the boat of the Christian community heading? It is following the direction set out by the Second Vatican Council, which laid out a roadmap, even though the road is not linear and the route needs continual adjusting. That is Francis's objective: he wants the Church to be the People of God, with Jesus at its heart, going forward highly attentive to the signs of the times.

Are the Vatican and structure of the hierarchy essential to the Church? And is there any solution to clericalism?

The Church existed for a long time without the structures familiar to us now, although I can't imagine Catholicism without ministers or a Petrine structure. The ministers draw the community together and keep the flame of faith alive. Of course, there are aberrations, which need eradicating, one of which, as the Pope says, is clericalism. It occurs when ministry is viewed as power and privilege, not as service, and the hierarchical structure is considered to be law that must be obeyed, regardless of people, times, or places. That was what happened to the Pharisees in the time of Jesus, and it can happen in the Church too.

The Pope often uses the image of the shepherd, which we usually link to the idea of leadership, although in the Gospels it's a bit more complex than that. Jesus asks us to be with each other like the shepherd willing to give up his life for his sheep. The idea of the Good Shepherd does not only refer to the relationship between the Bishop and his community but also to the relationships among the members of that community. However, a greater responsibility, involving the care of others, is laid on the minister. This can't be dispensed with. From that need to serve the community, through the preaching of the Word, the hierarchy is formed. It's interesting that the word *priest* is not used for ordained ministers in the New Testament, since it assures us that all the baptised are priests, prophets, and kings. The Letter to the Hebrews speaks of ministers of the word and service.

What do you see as the greatest challenges facing the Church at this time?

As the People of God on the move, the Church has a shared history, including of unprecedented situations, with the rest of humanity. The main point of tension involves keeping the focus always on mission because, as Paul VI said in his prophetic exhortation *Evangelii Nuntiandi*, the Church's raison d'être is its mission to proclaim the Gospel in all times, in all places. Our time is now, with the challenges and opportunities of today, even though we might wish the situation were different. It is in the here and now that the grace of God that sustains the mission of the Church is made manifest.

One issue now on the table is synodality, which will be explored in the next Synod of Bishops and which has also been discussed during previous synodal assemblies. We need to see these meetings as not just a meeting of hierarchs, but rather a time for the whole Church to be enlightened and return to its path inspired by the Spirit.

Another key issue is communication in the digital era. The mission of the Church, as I was saying, is to communicate the Gospel, but it needs to know how to do this in the world of today. This is one of the storms it must find a way through in order to learn how to communicate who we are. The prevailing image of the Church in the media is of the Pope or the hierarchy but not the People of God on the move. What should be expressed is the meaning of the Gospel as the source of reconciliation, peace, and hope, so that the Church is equipped to reach young people and other cultures. The Amazon Synod was a good example of this as it was conveyed in a very innovative fashion, through the diverse images of the people it represented, and how it was referred to inside and outside the meeting hall. We need to respond with greater boldness to the challenges of our time.

Is the Church today closer or further away from the dream that St. Ignatius held for her 500 years ago?

St. Ignatius's dream in his day was for the Church to be unified under the sign of the Cross and at the service of the Gospel. It is significant that the original formulation of the Society of Jesus (*Formula Instituti*, 1550) even then spoke of the reconciliation of mankind or "the estranged," to use the language of the day. Ignatius always felt united to the Church and particularly to the Pope, whom he referred to as the Vicar of Christ on Earth. Without this deep faith in Jesus, his dream would have proved impossible. St. Ignatius also wrote a little-known text, *Rules for Thinking with the Church*, which may evoke misunderstandings today as it reflects the mores of another era, but in this he deals with being emotionally and truly in tune with the Church, a key topic in the Spiritual Exercises.

Dreams arise from emotions, not reason, and in the case of Ignatius they derived from his connection with the Lord and with the Church. Both before and after his conversion, he was familiar with the intrigues and power games within the Christian community, since he was no ingenue and neither was he isolated from the world. Yet his experience of God and his faith led him to a place of radical fidelity. St. Ignatius was not just a dreamer but someone who tried to put into practice his dreams during a time that was particularly fraught due to the Reformation, Counter-Reformation and rather fluid boundaries between political and ecclesial power. It was an age of openness to the new world, with the discovery of America and Asia.

How do Jesuits today share that dream of St. Ignatius?

We who call ourselves, just like Ignatius, the companions of Jesus, still dream of a Church that is the spouse of Christ. The banner of the Cross is that of the One who was Crucified and Resurrected, rather than that of a tortured man or apparent failure. It is also the banner of the Easter experience. We dream of a Church united by a determination to make the Good News relevant, a Church passionate about incarnating the Gospel in every human culture and every area of our changing world today.

We also desire a Church that is completely independent of prevailing ideologies and stripped of political power, whose unity is nourished by the Lord, under the Petrine office of the Pontiff. That is the dream we have inherited from St. Ignatius. History will judge whether we are now closer or further away from making this a reality. Fortunately, the boundary between the Church and political power is not as fluid as it was in the time of Ignatius. One of the factors that makes the Holy Father a respected leader all over the world is the fact that he does not defend a political power structure. His power is that of the word, of witness, and mission. Pope Francis has always been very bold in dialogue with the world and with other Churches and religions. We are not in the same situation today as we were 500 years ago.

How is Francis's desire to have a Church committed to the peripheries changing the Christian community? And his desire for a Church that looks outward?

The Pope is encouraging trends, behaviours, and attitudes that already existed. Let's not forget that after being elected as

Bishop of Rome he said that the bishops had gone to the ends of the Earth to find him. This trend of shifting from the centre to the periphery, also seen with John Paul II, has been part of the Pope's own Christian journey. It was there while he lived out his vocation in his youth, during his time as a Jesuit, and in his witness as a bishop. Bergoglio has always perceived the need to set out for the peripheries, to abandon the well-trodden, usual paths, and to try and think things through in new ways. The need for this is more obvious than ever before in the change of era we are now going through.

The pandemic has accelerated everything, forcing us to embrace those processes that were already encouraging us to abandon our comfort zones and change the way we looked at society so that we may respond to needs that are now even more pressing. There are no ready-made answers, which is why we need to leave behind ideologies and clichés and methods that once seemed permanent and unchanging. We must embrace novelty, something very present in the Gospel. In fact, one of the most beautiful things in the Gospels is observing how Jesus breaks with convention, compelling others to do likewise. Some people laugh at him, others feel furious or threatened, but we all need to let go of our defenses. That is what a Church going forward means, that it's equipped to handle in, an unprecedented fashion, those unexpected situations that arise at the margins.

The Pope also advocates synodality. Can it work in all contexts?

Perhaps this is an easier idea to understand. "Synod" in Greek means walking together or being together on the road. The Second Vatican Council speaks of the People of God on the move, on a journey guided by the Spirit and following the Lord on his mission. The People of God, by its nature, is varied, as it comprises all the baptised. The word *lay* comes from the people. The Church is lay, and although different vocations may develop later within it, all rise up together to exercise the mission of proclaiming the Gospel.

Synodality is also associated with the journey and with the Church not being static. That is the great challenge: how to function as an ecclesial community in diverse contexts, as the Eucharist can be celebrated only in the community.

How does the Society of Jesus apply the principle of synodality?

It operates in a synodal fashion, functioning as a body in which decision making involves consulting the Spirit through all its members. The practice of consultation and an obligation to exercise this is common to all our structures: nobody takes decisions on a personal whim. The chief authority of the Society, the General Congregation, is an assembly in which different points of view are put forward. This reality contradicts the image of a vertical military structure sometimes associated with the Jesuits. The basis upon which we are organised is the opposite of an army.

Within the Society, it is understood that every member is involved in decision making: the role of the Superior is to place individuals in the best setting for them to develop the mission, not to tell them what they have to do. Furthermore, the destinations or missions assigned are chosen after a process of consultation. This will vary depending on the location and type of service involved, but many different voices are listened to, including that of the individual concerned. At the end of all the dialogue and shared process of discernment, the local superior or the provincial or the Father General, according to the specific circumstances, will have the last word. That is why accountability is so important in the Society, because as well as listening to what the Spirit is saying to the companion concerned, it also allows for the needs, weaknesses, and strengths of that Jesuit to be known, and therefore a decision to be reached about where he might be best placed to render the most assistance, given his gifts and bearing in mind his limitations.

Discernment is one of the most oft-repeated words of this pontificate. Do you think there is a real desire to open up this process within ecclesial institutions, or is this only a buzzword?

I find it striking that something so old can appear a novelty. Without discernment, there is no experience of God, and, just the same, we cannot speak of discernment without prayer. The most interesting Old Testament characters are people of discernment. And the great work of Jesus involves getting all of us to discern. He does not offer us ready-made answers but breaks down our constructs and discerns the truth with the Father from a place of common sense. Before taking any major decision, he first listens to God through prayer. Discernment allows us to be free from the law and, as St. Paul insists, to transcend it when it weighs on us like a yoke. The only law is our relationship with the Lord and charity: in the words of St. Augustine, "Love and do you what you want." St. Ignatius speaks of charity as "discreet" not because it is hidden but because it is love discerned. It is highly significant that whenever he suggested a rule in the Constitutions, he always did so saying that the times, individuals, and places involved should be taken into account. He leaves a wide margin for discretion. Our mission should take into account the specific times, individuals, and places where it takes place so that its essence can be effectively conveyed. Without such discernment, there is no Church and we become akin to a chain store trying to sell its wares.

For Francis, time is more important than space, which is why he intends to start processes ensuring that the changes he desires for the Church become irreversible. Do you think he is succeeding?

No other strategy is possible if we are to be true to Revelation, which starts with the incredibly inspiring story of Abraham. The Bible introduces him as a successful man, with a family and property, who plans for his future with great

Initiating processes involve walking down new paths without knowing where they'll lead you, opening up new horizons to allow the Holy Spirit to act.

serenity. But he encounters God, who asks him to leave everything and set off on a journey. That's what initiating processes involve: walking down new paths without knowing where they'll lead you, opening up new horizons to allow the Holy Spirit to act.

Francis contrasts the image of initiating processes to that of occupying spaces. Of course, this approach evokes insecurities, because as human beings we like things to be very clear and settled, but the fact is that experiencing God is destabilising. However, what brings me personally great peace is knowing that Jesus has promised in the Gospel that he will be with us always until the end of the world. If we rely on this security, then we can allow ourselves to be swept along, allowing God to guide us.

How to you interpret the Pope's phrase "stir things up"? What dangers might this entail?

The idea of initiating processes is more complex, while the phrase "stir things up" is one the Pope often uses with young people. It is an invitation to them to shun conformity and be fearless about bringing up the issues they are unhappy about. When a shakeup is imminent, the risk is that one becomes unsettled or looks for the answers elsewhere. In an ecclesial context, stirring things up means seeking the answers within synodality and not becoming a latter-day Savonarola who judges and condemns the church. Disquieting questions need to be asked in order to kickstart discernment among other reasons, but they shouldn't lead to a parallel Church. The Second Vatican Council represented a huge shakeup. Everything was carefully prepared beforehand, but then the Council took a different direction. The same thing happened with the Youth Synod, whose final emphases were very different from those set out at the start. That shakeup involved discernment and the search for answers as a group, as well as contemplating the changing signs of the times.

José Casanova, the Professor of Sociology at Georgetown University, has observed that the Pope has prompted the emergence of "prodigal son" syndrome among uber-zealous Catholics because, by going in search of the "lost son," he has neglected "the feelings of those who have stayed at home and been faithful."[6] Is that a view you share?

I love that parable because it completely unsettles me. The father does not only await the prodigal son but also goes in search of the older son, who gets upset when the return of his wastrel brother is celebrated. The father helps the older son to open up to the son who returns. The idea of the people who walked out being welcome when they return is fantastic. The house belongs to everyone and can be enlarged to fit in more people. This isn't an easy idea for every Christian, but the point is, staying at home doesn't make you the sole and exclusive owner of the house.

Do you understand why some Catholics criticise the Pope?

When Francis has made mistakes, he has had the courage to recognise and correct them and ask for forgiveness. That is quite normal in a synodal Church in which one seeks for truth alongside other people. That is why discernment and synods are necessary.

---

6 Interview published in *Vida Nueva* magazine, n. 3134 (15th–21st of June 2019), 39.

When you introduced the Universal Apostolic Preferences, you also observed that secularisation should be seen as a sign of the times through which the Spirit is challenging us today. What did you mean by that?

We need to distinguish between secularism and secularisation. The first, like any other "ism," is very aggressive and exclusionary. It is a battle against the sacred, the religious, and Church institutions. Secularisation, in contrast, is a process by which we need to learn to consider from a critical standpoint how religion can become an experience of God. What is termed "Christianity" in the Western world is more of a sociological phenomenon than a religious experience, i.e., you are Catholic because you were born into a Catholic family or in a Catholic country and you're part of that world. Secularisation leads you to question that in a process which, to my way of thinking at least, is healthy for the Church since it means that the experience of God is not confused with belonging to a particular tribe, race, nation, or people. In a secular environment, being Catholic is a decision that is down to every individual.

In a secular society, there is space for genuine religious freedom, for choosing if I do or do not want to be religious, and I am free to choose the religion I want. For the Church, this can be a plus, because this means that it will be made up of people who actually want to belong to her. That's where the missionary challenge arises: how to offer people a religious experience so that through this they can become part of this Church community. However, while it's true that the term *secularisation* may mean different things, it is generally understood to mean the separation of religion and state. In principle, that is not a problem either for the Church or for freedom of religion. However, when secularisation becomes a type of ideology, it can impose its own vocabulary and ideas that leave little space for true religious freedom.

How important is freedom when it comes to living out the faith?

Christianity requires people to be free to choose it. At the heart of the Christian faith is a personal relationship with Christ, which also takes an ecclesial form because the Christian faith needs and creates community. If we are to have a genuine relationship with God, then faith needs freedom. At its heart, it is always about a relationship of love, which in itself means freedom. In this sense, if society helps to free you from a religious experience that is akin to wearing a straitjacket, it can actually help you grow in faith.

As the Gospels show us, Jesus also sought to offer people that freedom. Often, we see him opposing the formal obligations imposed by religion because he recognised that they no longer fulfilled their purpose of helping people discover God and experience relationship with him as a true, lasting source of freedom. These obligations had become oppressive. They were experienced as obstacles blocking a straightforward, inclusive relationship with a merciful, compassionate Father, who can be known by us personally and who is available to everyone regardless of their circumstances or social status. Jesus destroyed images of God associated with structures of power and oppression. Setting this kind of religion free is a step towards an authentic faith in God.

Are we heading in Europe and the Americas towards a Catholic Church composed of a small, pure minority?

The Catholic Church is aware that it is made up of a community of fragile, sinful people who place themselves in the merciful hands of God so that they may be forgiven. For this reason, they cannot be considered pure. We need to be careful about purity as it can be the seed of religious fundamentalism, which is the worst of all kinds of fundamentalism because it kills in the name of God and sows intolerance in his name. There is no room for intolerance in the Church. Neither can God belong only to the pure.

I imagine that in the future the Church will be a community that is more conscious of its own ecclesiality because it will consist of people who have freely chosen to be part of it. I think there will be livelier, more diverse communities, overall and inside the Church, forming a Church that is more inculturated in local contexts, and which secularisation will have grounded in the here and now. This process fills me with optimism. We are heading for enrichment, and as the Pope says, towards a reality that is multi-faceted.

How should the Church adapt to the times without falling into the temptation of following fashion?

The Church shares the history of humankind, which is obviously changing. Her members today are not the same as those 500 years ago or in the time of St. Augustine, nor at the time when St. Peter and St. Paul came to Rome. She develops within specific historical contexts, which are subject to prevailing fashions and issues. Today, it behooves us to understand and respond to the situations evoked by the times we live in. That is what the Church has experience and tradition for, but that does not mean that she has ready-made answers for everything. Having a history is enriching, a source of help and inspiration, but it does not resolve every single problem that arises. That's why it is important to discern through the Spirit where the paths towards true life are leading in each era, unmasking and rejecting those that lead to superficiality or that destroy the human person. That same Spirit allows the Church to acknowledge the parts of its history that responded to a specific time period, but that invite us today to generate new responses, drawing on the same central message of Jesus.

Should the Church speak about politics?

Unfortunately, the word *politics* has acquired negative connotations, which makes me shudder, because nothing is as much connected to human life as politics. To live in our society, we need a decision-making structure, which is why it is completely absurd to contemplate humanity without politics. As it is made up of human beings, there are politics in the Church too, both internally and in relationship to society at large. That does not mean there should be no boundaries between political and religious power. The Pope's last encyclical, *Fratelli Tutti*, reflects on this wonderful vision of us all being jointly responsible for the common good, which is why humanity cannot exist without politics.

Christians are also citizens, and we have to engage with the common good, not just worry about it, which is why the Church cannot stop having an active voice

Christians are also citizens, and we have to engage with the common good, not just worry about it.

in public life. No one argues over whether Caritas, the Church's relief and development agency, should provide food for the needy, but it seems to be a surprise when the Church, inspired by exactly the same awareness of human rights, opposes a law it considers unjust. If we don't take part in public life, we will be pure, yes, but pure "idiots" as those who evaded their political or civic duties through placing self-interest above the interests of society, were known in ancient Greece. We do not want a Church of "idiots" but one that leads us to be better, more political citizens, who take care of others and of the common good. That is why we speak so much about justice, reconciliation, and peace.

You are the president of the Union of Superiors General (USG) of the masculine religious congregations. How do you see the present and the future for consecrated life?

Its future depends on our experience of God and our trust in him through others. That is why in the tradition of the Church there are so many forms of consecration: all involve men and women who place God at the centre of their lives and relate to him through prayer and contemplation. They commit, furthermore, to being detached from all possessions, choosing to do so via the channel of obedience to others. Many ways to live out this witness exist, whether in the contemplative life, as a catechist in a parish, as a nurse in a hospital, or as a teacher in a school. The kind of service involved in the life of religious can be quite varied. Whatever its virtues and failings, it's necessary for the Church, although at the same time, also dispensable. The definition of the Church would not change much according to whether it does or doesn't have religious. However, within the ecclesial community there have always been some people who have received a call from the Spirit to live for God in a specific way and who try to follow within this call the same choices made by Jesus.

What does the life of religious bring to the Church?

Not all of us are called to it, but it does the Church a great deal of good. Male and female religious bring a freedom through discernment to place themselves completely in the hands of God, as well as a willingness to go to wherever they are needed. Thus, they live out the radical nature of the Gospel message, in tune with prophetic tradition. They are in the front line of those who are willing to be sent on mission, to take care of people others do not take care of, as Mother Teresa of Calcutta said, or of those who do not take care of others full time, as is the case with many monastic orders and congregations devoted to a life of praise and contemplation. In the Church's past and today, the Spirit continues to inspire the founding of a vast diversity of institutes, groups, and communities, which include differing degrees of secular and apostolic outreach.

On what basis should we build a relationship with non-believers?

A Church on the move relates in full freedom to all human beings, with whom she shares a common history and seeks to partner to attain the common good. The believer offers their faith, which is what inspires them and may be accepted by others. The key lies in the freedom, as much of the believer who is open about their life of faith, as that of the non-believer, who becomes open to relationship without feeling pressured. What is persuasive is witness. A clear distinction needs to be made between proselytism and evangelisation, which makes an offer [of faith] but does not oblige or impose. That is the difference between the individual who freely chooses to be Christian and Christianity being imposed for cultural or social reasons.

How can religions contribute to creating peace and fraternity, as the Encyclical Fratelli Tutti suggests?

The experience of God can spur human beings to seek peace and fraternity. There are many ways of seeking God, not just Christianity. At one point, the Catholic Church thought she was the only option. That is no longer the case today. That is one of the great learning points of the previous centuries. Inter-religious dialogue helps us attain fraternity among cultures and individuals, although this can be explored only to the degree that religions are true to themselves and lead to an openness to others. *Fratelli Tutti* should be read alongside the earlier Abu Dhabi declaration: *A document on human fraternity for world peace and living together.*

Where do you think Pope Francis's concern to foster inter-religious dialogue comes from?

It has at least two sources, one being Vatican II, which opened up new possibilities for inter-religious dialogue and, later on, an awareness of how religions have been used to legitimise violence. If world religions can help us better understand and deepen our sense of a shared humanity, that we all share a deep spiritual quest, then they can be a source of peace and reconciliation instead of excuses for violence and destruction. The Pope thinks that this is an urgent task in our fragile and precarious world. Every religion here has a moral obligation to serve all humanity by constructing peace and legitimising the profound desire of the human spirit that *Fratelli Tutti* may serve as a kind of "roadmap" for this process. At the same time, we're able to recognise that the hindrance to peace is not our differences. One of the great learning points of the past century is that the more we commit ourselves to this dialogue, the more we become able to appreciate our own faith. Inter-religious dialogue helps to achieve fraternity among cultures and individuals, but it can be addressed only to the extent that religions are true to their own identity and open towards each other.

What role can inter-religious dialogue play in fighting religious fundamentalism?

Dialogue helps, but first of all you have to look at yourself and visit your own sources of inspiration. Dialogue begins with knowing who you are. This obliges the Church and other religions to be true to their own identities. That is the best way to combat fundamentalism, which in my opinion is the ultimate expression of ideology. Any religion can be perverted to the point where it turns into fundamentalism. That is a danger from which Catholicism is not exempt. It also exists today within the Church, and I imagine it will do so in the future because many people still feel comfortable adopting fundamentalist attitudes.

What is your personal experience within this field?

I have been influenced as much by personal experiences as by a group created by Adolfo Nicolas, comprising various Jesuits who work in ecumenism, alongside the Eastern Churches, and in dialogue with Islam, Buddhism, Judaism, and indigenous religions. We meet once a year to address a specific topic from our individual perspectives. In 2020, the question we explored was how world religions had handled the pandemic. It was very interesting, and it made me more aware of the variety of religious perspectives and the possibility of attaining common ground. We should not forget that the majority of Jesuits work today in settings where Christianity is not the majority religion.

Can ecumenical dialogue help to promote conversion among Christians?

Of course. In all this it is good to start with those of our own faith family. All the traditions which shape the Christian faith are also the product of our history. Now, however, we have the desire and the urgent need to "heal our memories" and, in the name of Jesus, put aside our prejudices and fears, our divisions and the ways in which they can be used challenge us. How can we call ourselves Christians, but fail to be united? In the Gospel of John, Jesus, from the depth of his very self, prays in the presence of the Father, "that they may all be one" (John 17:20–26). We should certainly listen to and respond to this prayer of the one Lord common to us all.

Would the theological unity of Christians involve us all becoming the same?

No. It would involve us all sharing the same bread. Unfortunately, that is not something I see happening anytime soon, although I recognise the prevalence of good will from all parties concerning this. I find it hard to understand why Christians are not united, especially because when one examines history, one sees that sometimes our ruptures were the result of misunderstandings, cultural differences, or power dynamics, which then became entrenched over time. It is sad that we have not been able to overcome such things. The encyclical *Fratelli Tutti* defines in very beautiful language the meaning of dialogue: to draw close to one another, to express ourselves, to listen to each other, to look at each other, to know each other, to try to understand each other and to find points of contact... the Pope suggests that dialogue is a culture, so that those verbs may be enacted. All this should lead to communion, which is the ultimate objective of all ecumenical dialogue.

"TO SERVE THE LORD ALONE AND THE CHURCH, HIS SPOUSE"[7]

In the autumn of 1910, the Spanish artist Pablo Picasso completed a portrait of his friend and representative in Paris, Daniel-Henry Kahnweiler. In the picture, countless small pieces, of differing shades and tonalities, intermingle to discreetly reveal a recognisable image of Kahnweiler, albeit one translucent with elements of his surroundings. The painting represents very different attributes and perspectives of the subject, which the viewer connects with according to their sensibility, yet none obscure the person depicted. It is he who lends the whole unity and meaning. This might be useful for us as an image of the Church, the work of the Spirit, who interweaves pieces that do not appear to fit together, being of differing shapes and tonalities, some very similar to their surroundings, some being shiny, others dark but which overall, if from different perspectives, allow us to clearly see Jesus Christ, who provides the whole with unity and meaning. The Church has been represented in many ways throughout history: as a boat in the eye of the storm, through St. Paul's image of a body, and as the field hospital to which Pope Francis refers. These are complementary images yet do not exhaust the riches of the Spirit nor cease to witness to Christ in the centre of the world. A Church on pilgrimage, a Church on the move, a Church that proclaims the Gospel.

---

7 From the *Formula of the Institute* approved by Julius III (1550). https://bit.ly/3pzPqj6.

PRAYER POINTS

Composition of place. Think of some pictures that evoke your sense of belonging to the Church.

Grace to ask for. Lord, may I grow in love for your Church and offer my gifts to serve you through her.

First point. Think of the communities of faith and hope in which your love for God has flourished and where you have found "true friends in the Lord." Give thanks for them and draw spiritual benefit from this.

Second point. Think about situations that involve borders, physical or existential, that are being transformed into invitations for the Church today. List them and allow your feelings and desires about these situations to arise within you.

BIBLE TEXTS

Mark 4:35–41 / 1 Corinthians 12

» How do you experience your membership of the Church? How do you feel that God is calling you to be Church today?

» Which storms does the Church still need to navigate? What sparks our doubt and uncertainty in the Church? What can you do to ensure that the Church's gaze is fixed on Jesus and that her modus operandi reflects the power of the Spirit?

» What talents can you bring to the Church so that you may be a pilgrim alongside others within her? How are you living out the call to Synodality, to the complementarity of ecclesial experiences, as a witness to concord and fraternity?

Colloquy. Tell Jesus about the light and the darkness you have experienced within the Church, and let him tell you of his dreams for the People of God. Finish with an Our Father and a Hail Mary. Do not forget to examine what you have experienced during this prayer time.

TIPS FOR SPIRITUAL CONVERSATION

For spiritual conversation that arises from personal prayer, the following steps from the general methodology of spiritual conversation are recommended (p. 268).

For spiritual conversation concerning an apostolic work, the following prayer points may be beneficial.

Composition of place. Recall the ways in which the Church, implicitly or explicitly, is present in the apostolic work or mission with which I am cooperating.

Grace to ask for. Lord, may we be able to witness to the communion to which you call us, in our apostolic activity and as a Church.

Bible text. 1 Corinthians 12. How are we forming an apostolic body for mission in the situation we find ourselves in? Are we bearing witness to fraternity, complementarity, and mutual edification? Are our spaces of mission and cooperation encouraging? Do they allow everyone to use the gifts they have received from God? Are we working towards creating communion with the local Church? If so, how? And what more could we do?

Colloquy. Tell Jesus about the challenges you face and the gifts you desire to place at the service of greater ecclesial communion. Finish with an Our Father and a Hail Mary. Do not forget to examine what you have experienced during the prayer time. The fruits of the prayer can be shared according to the steps of the general methodology for spiritual conversation.

"Wherever in the Church, even in the most difficult and extreme fields, in the crossroads of ideologies, in the front line of social conflict, there has been and there is confrontation between the deepest desires of man and the perennial message of the Gospel, there also there have been, and there are, Jesuits."

Paul VI, December 3rd, 1974

5 The Society of Jesus Today

Union of hearts and minds. Roy M. Thottam, SJ

The Society's General Congregations (GC) and several Popes have, in different ways, articulated the mission of the institute. How has the order been shaped by this process between the time of Paul VI and Francis?

We need to understand this process within the context of the Church: without her, there would be neither the Society of Jesus nor Popes. Our order was conceived as a group of people at the service of the Church who followed the voice of the Pope. That is why what he says has such a tremendous impact on the life of the Society. In this sense, the Second Vatican Council was an exceptional context. One of the great historic landmarks of the Church, it triggered processes that had a deep repercussion on our institution. With Vatican II, the Church and the Popes insisted on reading the signs of the times and responding to them. That is the process we have been living through for the past almost 60 years.

It's fascinating to see how the General Congregations of the Society of Jesus evolved between the 31st GC (1965) and the 36th (2016); each tried to read the signs of the times and listen to the voice of the Church through the Pope. GC31, which was held in 1965, saw Pedro Arrupe chosen as the successor to the Superior General, Jean-Baptiste Janssens, who had died the previous year, but after that the sessions were suspended and did not re-convene again until after the Council. That gave Fr. Arrupe and the Society time to prepare for the reception of Vatican II, for which many Jesuits had worked as periti.[8]

---

8 Theological advisors to the Council.

GC 31 opened with Paul VI's remarkable speech asking the order to tackle atheism. What kind of impact did his words have?

The Pope revealed the change that was taking place in the Church and sparked a very profound theological reflection. This contributed to a renewal of thinking about the Church from the inside and led to a stronger emphasis on the social sciences. The Society joined this with enthusiasm. In those years, which overlapped with my formation as a Jesuit, there was tremendous interest in understanding the phenomenon we now call secularisation. This led to a fresh understanding of the evolution of society and to the renewal of theological thinking. It was around this time that Liberation Theology emerged in Latin America as well as in India and Africa. There was an explosion of spiritual and theological creativity and in the application of social sciences.

That process led Arrupe to call GC32 in 1975, ten years after the end of the Second Vatican Council. General Congregations are held by the Society not only to elect a new Superior General. He may also request at specific times that a General Congregation is held to allow for discernment of the mission. GC32 picked up on all the energy in thought and deed inspired by the Council to articulate that the promotion of the faith and seeking justice were core to our mission. At that GC, the Society was defined for the first time on paper, at least as far I know, as a body of sinners who have been forgiven and who are called to participate in the mission of Christ. This is what has defined the Society's mission ever since then. It is important that we are aware of the fragility of who we are and what we do. That meeting also led a drive towards inculturation.

After GC33, held in 1983, which saw the election of Peter-Hans Kolvenbach as General, came GC34 in 1995. In contrast to the previous GC, this was topic-based. How did the Society of Jesus then change its direction?

It confirmed our focus on the promotion of faith and justice and dialogue with other cultures and religions. It introduced the idea of us being not only *for* others but *with* others, that we are all partners and servants in the mission of Christ. Another key concern to emerge from that General Congregation was ecology. A decree regarding the place of women in the Church was also approved, and this is something we plan to go into in greater depth.

The next General Congregation, the 35th, held in 2008, saw the election of Adolfo Nicolás and introduced the issue of reconciliation in three areas: with God, among people, and with the environment. The 36th General Congregation held in 2016 explored this line of thinking further by considering how the purpose of each one of our dimensions is, to quote St. Paul, the reconciliation of all things in Christ. That is the aim of our work: to promote faith and seek justice. GC36 also highlighted the question of partnership with others. The mission was understood from then on in more complex terms, as meaning that the mission of the Society is part of the mission that Christ has entrusted to the Church. This connects us to the very roots of the order and to a document that the Church sometimes forgets: Paul VI's Apostolic Exhortation *Evangelii Nuntiandi*, the text which expresses most clearly the ecclesiology of the Second Vatican Council.

Why did the Society of Jesus need the new Universal Apostolic Preferences (UAPs) approved in February 2019? What was new about them and the process of collating them?

The UAPs are the result of GC36, which asked for some preferences to be established based on the existing ones. What was really new was the process we used to work them out. The first UAPs emerged in 2003 in response to a request that the GC34 made to the then Superior General, Peter-Hans Kolvenbach, to set out some priorities for us, as it is impossible to cover everything. The process of defining them took nearly ten years and did not, at least on a formal level, involve everyone in the Society.

The inception of the new UAP dates from 2014, when Nicolás summoned GC36, which happened two years later. By then, the concerns of the Province Congregations, which took place in 2015, had emerged. Then, during the General Congregation itself, which involved a great deal of community discernment, a request was made for the whole order to be included in the reflection process, as well as the non-Jesuits involved in our missionary activity. So that is exactly what we did. It was a very enriching process that lasted two years, involving communities, institutions, provinces, regional conferences, the General Curia, and the Pope.

The greatest initial impact of the UAPs was the process we used to work them out: an understanding that decision making follow widespread discernment. The influence of this was obvious in some of the decisions made after their approval. Personally speaking, I'm very happy with how the journey to pin down the UAP evolved. We were not following any kind of instruction manual and had to make it up as we went along. It was beautiful to witness the enthusiasm, seriousness, and creativity that all the Jesuits and non-Jesuits involved brought to the process.

Later, we will discuss each UAP, but I want to just mention now that I don't understand why, given that education is so important to the Society of Jesus, it was not included in the Preferences. Why was that?

The UAPs are not apostolic areas or activities but rather guidelines that inspire everything the Society does. They are guidelines for the lifestyle and mission we should adopt in all our apostolic activities. These UAPs were not designed in the same way as those formulated by Fr. Kolvenbach in 2003. Then, the main concern was to define our priorities in the light of our diminishing human and apostolic resources. Fr. Kolvenbach did not say what needed to be closed down or left open. Instead, he listed five universal apostolic necessities which required a communal effort from the body of the Society.

Those we have now are based on a different approach. These are guidelines that emerged from a process of discernment at every level and that work like the five fingers of a hand. The fifth finger is partnership with others, while the wrist, which ensures all the fingers are working, is the Holy Spirit. Our challenge now is to assimilate all the UAP into our life of mission. Education, for instance, should be given by attending to the voice of the Spirit, by fostering discernment, and through the Spiritual Exercises, but it should also respond to the cry of the poor, the young, and the environment. This will naturally take a different guise in parishes, communities, social centres, or retreat houses, but what must be present in all these contexts is a commitment to the four dimensions of the UAP.

The earlier preferences included China and Africa. Neither are mentioned in the current UAP. Has the Society's interest in those regions diminished?

The new UAPs, which will be rolled out between 2019 and 2029, certainly do not mean that we are abandoning our interest in the work of global mission set out in the previous preferences. Africa today is the place where the Apostolic body of the Society is seeing the most growth, as much in vocations as in our activities and partnerships. Many of the great challenges of the world, including racism, multi-culturalism, interculturality, and the thoughtless exploitation of nature, are concentrated in this territory, whose cultural riches are so plentiful. The youngest of the continents, it has a great spiritual tradition. Africa is certainly of immense value for humankind.

What can you tell us about the Society's mission in China?

It is still extremely challenging, but we have a group of Jesuits there. Not a very big one, but a significant presence nonetheless. In the last three decades, a wave of Jesuits has gone to China, Taiwan, Hong Kong, and Macao, the territories that comprise the province. Some of the vocations in this region over the past twenty years have come from China. We're talking of small numbers, but they represent significant growth nonetheless. This demonstrates that inculturation in Chinese society is happening. The Society has found creative ways to make its presence felt within the complex political and social world of China. It has a very strong partnership with the open faith community, to whom the Jesuits offer an apostolate typical of the Society, e.g. The Spiritual Exercises and opportunities for discernment. There are no schools there, but there are centres of alternative education, including the Beijing Centre for Chinese Studies, which is located in a local university that promotes academic and cultural interchange between China and the rest of the world. Furthermore, several Jesuits teach in Chinese state universities. Also significant is our indirect presence in this region through the Chinese men and women who study at the Society's universities abroad, mainly in the United States. They tend to end up working later in important institutions in China, so their formation has an impact on Chinese society.

What do you imagine the Society of Jesus will be like in twenty years?

A far more complex and intercultural Apostolic body, which has spread to every continent, yet is well connected and capable of shared discernment. St. Ignatius used the expression "the least Society" but he did not mean numerically: he was referring to humility, to being subordinate to the service of the Church and evangelisation. This idea of being "least" I also imagine will apply to the location of the order in the future and its partnership with others. There will be fewer Jesuits numerically, but of more varied cultural origin, and they will work on joint activities or projects instigated by other people, thus ensuring a greater integration of resources within the Church and the Society of Jesus. I also hope that the balance of Jesuit brothers to Jesuit priests will be better. I sincerely hope that there will be more vocations to be Jesuit brothers than is the case at present.

What do you think Jesus and St. Ignatius would say today to you and to the Society?

Jesus would say to us, "Follow me." Those are the words that I hear constantly. He would also remind us that he is with us every day, and he would urge us not to forget that he has given us the Holy Spirit, who reminds us of what Jesus said to us and explains how we should be doing what he asked of us today.

With regard to St. Ignatius, I think he would say, "Only he who has deigned to begin this work in us can bring it to completion." That is something he repeated often: this work is of God, and only he can complete it. That is why the most important thing for a Jesuit is to stay united to God and to be an instrument of his mission.

> **The most important thing for a Jesuit is to stay united to God and to be an instrument of his mission.**

How many Jesuits are there today? Where are most new vocations coming from? Are you worried by the decrease in numbers?

The Society has around 15,000 members: around 11,000 are priests, 1,000 are brothers, 700 are novices, and 2,400 are scholastics, who have already finished their novitiate and are finishing further studies. Most of our vocations come from Africa and South Asia. But there are other variables: in the USA, Europe, and Australia, the numbers of new entrants are lower, but they tend to be older and have more qualifications. Social patterns vary in different places, and maturity does not occur at the same age in every single country.

The decrease in numbers does not worry me so much as whether we are promoting vocations to the kind of religious life the Society desires. It has a very specific style, devised by Ignatius and his companions, which is quite unlike other kinds of religious life. Another worry is whether there is a real openness to partnership in our missions so that we do not always have to be at the head of all the apostolic works we run. And then there is the great challenge of formation for all who partner in the mission of the Church to be at the service of humanity.

What does it bring to the Society of Jesus to have Jesuit brothers as well as Jesuit priests?

Just like St. Paul, St. Ignatius often used the image of the body. All the organs are necessary for the body to exist and function overall. The Society is a body of people united through their religious consecration, their vows, and their response to being called to exercise different roles within the Church. The lay consecrated vocation of a Jesuit brother and the vocation to ordained ministry of the priest mutually enhance each other. Together, they form the Society's style of religious life. These two vocations create a way of life centred upon the individual's consecration within the Society and to the mission of the Church, to which he can contribute in many different ways. There are no first- or second-class Jesuits. A Jesuit brother is as much a member of the Society as is a Jesuit priest. A vocation is defined by the one who calls you: the Lord. Neither vocation is better than the other. This is a gift for the order and for the

Church. Sometimes, the vocation of the Jesuit brother needs protecting from external pressures. I have known Jesuits who have had to fight for their vocation as brothers because their families, friends, or milieu were pressuring them to become priests. They are excellent Jesuits who contribute their own quite unique qualities to the mission. Any function within the Society for which the Church does not demand priestly orders can be carried out by a brother. They can be university rectors, school headmasters, or directors of social centres for instance, but not parish priests.

How would you explain the process of interior conversion that the Society of Jesus also desires to see within its institutions?

This is something that goes far deeper than being up-to-date or adjusting to changing circumstances, which for an institution implies having the latest programs, technology, or facilities. It means being open to the work of God in individuals, communities, and institutions. The image of Pentecost helps us grasp this. After the death of Jesus, the disciples were frightened more than anything else and went into hiding, but through Pentecost they became open to the work of the Spirit and changed into people of great courage and creativity. They were then able to start a movement in the very tough circumstances of their era, in the Jewish society of the time, then under the domination of the Roman Empire. That is conversion, which for an institution, involves accepting that it is only a means to fulfil a mission rather than an end in itself. That awareness can occasionally lead to an institution closing down because it's no longer possible to maintain it or it's no longer efficient in apostolic terms or because a decision has been made to devote the resources available to something else. In order to be more efficient, the Society can and must change the methods and structures it uses to develop its mission.

The protection of minors is one of the greatest problems the Church faces today. How has this affected the Society of Jesus?

It has been a huge shake-up as much for the Church in general as for the Society in particular. We have learnt a great deal since the first cases began to emerge in countries including the United States or Ireland nearly thirty years ago now. The biggest learning point has been changing our focus: previously our concerns centred on ourselves. Now our whole focus is on the victims. Learning to hurt for the victims has been our biggest lesson. But there is still a long way to go.

In what sense?

Just as in the political sphere, we speak of reparative justice; work needs to be done in this field to ensure that more is done beyond just the application of juridical and canonical penalties. We should try to seek to right the relationship with the person who has been victimized. From the standpoint of our faith, we should aim to reach a place of reconciliation and forgiveness, although this is extremely hard to do.

At the last General Congregation, it was recommended that we develop a culture of safeguarding. We do not just need to know how to deal with these cases or how to try and avoid them. We must also create safe environments where interaction with other people does not put minors or vulnerable people at risk.

This requires developing a high degree of human and cultural maturation as the Pope insists in *Fratelli tutti*.

Are the days of cover-up over for the Jesuits? What has your personal experience with this issue been?

We have switched on the light in a very dark room, but the light has not yet reached every single corner. We are on a learning curve. As I was saying, our focus is now the victims, we have developed safeguarding procedures, and we are beginning to understand what reparative justice means. But we still have a great deal more to do. We also need to learn to how to try to rescue the perpetrators, who are our brothers. I only began to hear about this issue when I was Provincial in Venezuela and heard about the cases in the United States. We had several meetings for joint reflection with the US provincials, who told us about their experiences in this field, but in my province at that time I did not have to deal with any cases. Here in Rome, as the Superior General of the Society, I handle a good number of cases coming from every continent.

What do you do now with Jesuits who are abusers?

First of all, they must complete their sentence. If they are in prison, we visit them to try and help them get through this as well as possible, as one would do with a brother. If they are under canonical penalty, they must also complete the full sentence, but often the individual concerned will remain in the community house. If he is a priest, all his ministerial activity is suspended. If he is a brother, the same applies to his public activity. However, you can't put these individuals in the deep freeze: some kind of service needs to be found for them. There are many tasks they can do, e.g., helping out in the library or with the sick. But it is not just about them being able to do something: above all, they must go through a process within the context of a fraternal community. It is one thing to accept a sentence. It is quite another and far more difficult to accept the truth, to see what must change in order for the individual to try and recover and reach a place of truly asking for and being able to receive forgiveness. During this process, one discovers that many abusers were abused themselves during childhood. Ultimately, you are dealing with people who need to be healed. The challenge lies in creating the right conditions for this to happen.

Is the Society responsible for paying compensation to the victims?

Yes, that is part of our responsibility. There are various ways of doing this, which depend on the individual situation, but normally we would cover all the cost of psychotherapy and whatever is necessary to help the victim find employment and start their life over. Something that surprises me is that however much is done, with very few exceptions, a lingering sense of dissatisfaction remains. The pain and the bitterness remain. It is very hard to move on. That is why it is important to find a way forward that leads to forgiveness and reconciliation.

What does its fourth vow of obedience to the Pope mean for the Society of Jesus today?

It means being available for the mission of Jesus through the Church, as made manifest through the Petrine office. For the Society, the voice of the Pope defines our mission, and the vow of obedience means being available for this. It is simply a vow to be sent by him on mission wherever the Church needs us to go. From the time of the first companions of Ignatius, this ensured that the Society's limited resources could be directed towards the greatest universal good, which since he has a universal vision of the Church, is defined by the Bishop of Rome. Since the Society wishes to place itself at the service of the greatest universal good, it chooses to be guided by the voice of the Pope. That is where the vote of obedience, which has a practical rather than a solely theological rationale, comes from.

Do you understand the controversies surrounding Fr. Arrupe?

Pedro Arrupe needs to be understood within the historical context where he developed his mission. As a young missionary in Japan, he experienced the horror of the atomic bomb in Hiroshima. Later, as Superior General, **Arrupe had the courage to be faithful.** he had to grapple with the upheaval of Vatican II. It is remarkable that in such complex situations he was able, as the Jesuits acknowledge, to exercise a kind of universal leadership. He allowed himself to be guided by the Spirit and not only allowed but in fact encouraged creativity. I don't believe the controversies came from or were due to Arrupe personally but rather that they emanated from the Church as a whole in a time of great turbulence. Arrupe had the courage to be faithful to what the Second Vatican Council and the Society were asking of him. That is how the tensions with the Vatican Curia in the time of Paul VI may be understood.

At what stage is his process of beatification?

It's very much on track. Many of us, both Jesuits and other religious and Christians, regard Fr. Arrupe as an inspirational figure who had an aura of holiness. Devotion to him has been growing since his time as Superior General. During the ten years he spent in great suffering in the infirmary after having a stroke, no Jesuit or indeed any other person who had the chance to do so would fail to visit him whenever they came to Rome. Many people found him an inspiration, as can be seen through the large number of Jesuit institutions bearing his name. For the Jesuits, he is a person of profound significance. That is why we decided to start the cause for his beatification, which is on the right track, despite being delayed by the pandemic. I hope that in 2021 we will be able to present the *positio* to the Congregation for the Causes of Saints.

Decades ago, some people saw the Society of Jesus almost as "a parallel Church." Does that danger remain today? Does anyone still call the Society the Black Pope?

I ask for forgiveness if at any time we may have seemed like a parallel Church. That runs completely counter to the Society's *raison d'être*, as from its beginning it has known that it was subordinate to the one and only Church. That is why Jesuits renounce any aspiration to be a Bishop or hold any other form of ecclesiastical office. To avoid giving anyone reasons for seeing us as a parallel Church, we need to remain faithful to our charism. The expression *black pope* disquiets me and seems to me to be totally absurd. I won't even use it as joke. It has as its origin an attempt to damage the Society and the Church by suggesting a supposed parallel between their level of authority. There is only one Pope, and whoever truly wishes to respect the Church cannot accept that expression, which distorts the true likeness of the Bishop of Rome and of the Superior General of the order.

What are the advantages and disadvantages for the Society of Jesus in having a Pope who is a Jesuit? What kind of relationship do you and the Pope have with each other?

No one ever thought there would be a Jesuit Bishop of Rome. For the Society, in any case, the Pope is the Pope whatever his background and whoever he is. The fact that the Pope is now a Jesuit places us at a disadvantage because he has to be careful not to give the impression that he has a preferential relationship with the Society.

Pope Francis and I have a very amiable and fraternal relationship. But that's not just how he is with me. That's how he is. Our relationship is also one of great respect. He does not try to intervene in Society matters, but that does not prevent his being always very willing to help whenever we consult him, and vice versa. Neither those in governance in the Society nor I try ever try to take advantage of the fact that a Jesuit is now Bishop of Rome. We have a healthy relationship. We do not see each other too often or with particular regularity. During the process of preparing the UAPs, I did go to see him every three months to update him, but now we see each other at public occasions or if a specific issue requires us to meet.

Do you consult each other over decisions? Do you ever tell the
Pope if you think he's made a mistake about something?

I try to raise only essential matters with him. Sometimes
I might ask him what he thinks about an issue, and I'll give
him my opinion about specific questions if he asks me for it.
That happened with Adolfo Nicolás too. The Pope can call me
whenever he wants, but to contact him I use the same channels
as anyone else. I have to contact his secretary first. I don't have
direct access to him.

I imagine the election of Jorge Maria Bergoglio as Pope was
a surprise to many Jesuits because he had taken a step back from
the Society of Jesus. In addition, he had his differences with
Kolvenbach. What can you tell us about that relationship?

His election was a huge surprise: because he was a Jesuit,
because he was Latin American, and even because of his age.
When his appointment was announced, there was a degree of
uncertainty over the kind of relationship a Jesuit Pope who had
been a bishop for a long time might have with the Society of
Jesus. Bergoglio broke the tension himself by telephoning the
curia of the order to speak to Fr. Nicolás and invite him to a
meeting. After that they had a really good relationship. In fact,
they were contemporaries, only a few months apart. In a certain
sense, I inherited that very fraternal relationship. Our impression is that the Holy Father feels at home when he comes to our
curia, as he does at least once a year to lunch with us in July
to celebrate the feast of St. Ignatius. Regarding the relationship
between Bergoglio and Kolvenbach I have nothing to say. What
a Jesuit discusses with his Superior General is absolutely private.

What was it like for you when the Jesuit Juan Antonio Guerrero was named "finance minister" at the Vatican?

It was like undergoing an amputation, and having my right arm chopped off. That is what I said both to the Pope and to Guerrero, who had been my right hand in an important mission: the management of the houses and interprovincial works of the Society in Rome. This is not straightforward, and Guerrero had taken on the task with great responsibility and flair. Francis was seeking a specific individual for this mission. It wasn't a case of him asking the Society to take charge of the Vatican finances. The Pope gathered information because he was searching for someone he could trust for the job and landed on Guerrero. I encouraged him to meet Guerrero in person. They met, and later the Pope confirmed he was going to name him minister. And that was that.

"WITH A HEART STRETCHED TOWARDS THE INFINITY OF GOD"

"In a book published in 1640, an author set himself the task and created this maxim: *Non coerceri a maximo, contineri tamen a minimo, hoc divinum est.* Translating that is not very easy, but the sense is this: "To be unconstrained by the greatest, to be contained even in the slightest-this is the divine." To put that into our perspectives: to live in the dimension of the universal, yet to labor on the concrete particular, this is the divine. This is the mystery of Christ, because he who is the "greatest" above and beyond every conceivable frontier border, the unconstrainable Majesty of God, the divine Majesty that nothing can force or impede is found in the "least," in the flesh and heart of the Incarnate Word, in a precise place in the Roman empire, in a precise time during human history. In this vision of Christ's mystery, Ignatius adopts a line of conduct: following Christ, to immerse oneself in concrete work according to one's opportunities and one's abilities, but single-heartedly straining towards the infinity of God, who presents in the here and now the wide horizons of his plan of salvation."

PRAYER POINTS

Preparatory prayer. Ask the Lord our God for grace that all my intentions, actions and operations may be directly purely to the service and praise of his Divine Majesty. [*Ex* 46; cf. *Ex* 23].

Grace to ask for. Lord, grant me your Spirit so that I may be moved by the Universal Apostolic Preferences and be willing to love you and follow you through them.

First point. Remember in gratitude and with hope all the different Jesuits who have worked in different areas and who you think gave or are giving everything for the greater glory of God wherever they have been sent on mission. Reflect on this and draw spiritual benefit.

BIBLE TEXTS

» **Mark 10:46–52.** The blind man in the Gospel wants to see and knows he will only manage to do so if he reaches Jesus, so he shouts out repeatedly until he reaches him. Is Jesus the one who helps you to have a broad outlook and courageous desires? What nourishes your longings, desires and hopes?

» **Matthew 13:31–33.** The tininess of the seed does not prevent it from later providing others with shelter and support. How do you experience your daily surrender? Have you experienced that call to give yourself in small, daily things, but with a heart open to the infinity of God? What has this experience been like? How do you experience today this creative tension between what is local and what is universal in mission?

» **John 15:1–5.** It is only by abiding in the one who calls that our mission becomes fruitful. Apply this text to your life, vocation and present mission. Where is it calling you?

Finish the prayer. If you feel moved to do so, pray to the *Eternal Lord of all things* that if it is his will, your gifts may serve to reflect his face in our history, in everything from the small and everyday to the large and spectacular. End with an Our Father and a Hail Mary. Do not forget to examine what you have experienced during this prayer time.

TIPS FOR SPIRITUAL CONVERSATION

For spiritual conversation that arises from personal prayer, the following steps from the general methodology of spiritual conversation are suggested (p. 268).

For spiritual conversation concerning an apostolic work, the following prayer points may be beneficial.

Grace to ask for. Lord, grant me your spirit that I might embrace the Universal Apostolic Preferences, and through them recognise your call in our apostolic mission.

Bible text. Luke 4:16–22. What is the Spirit calling us to today? Who are the poor, the oppressed, those in need of liberation, and who around us reveals God to us through their actions and witness? Where are they leading us?

Colloquy. Ask Mary, our Mother to obtain for you the grace from the Father to be open to his Spirit. Finish with an Our Father and a Hail Mary. Do not forget to examine what you have experienced during the prayer time. The fruits of the prayer can be shared according to the steps of the general methodology for spiritual conversation.

Finding God in daily life lies at the heart of the human adventure. The Society of Jesus fosters this encounter with the Lord in contemporary society through the Spiritual Exercises, Discernment, and the Ignatian Examen.

6 Showing the Way to God

"And what if God spoke to you? What would he tell you?" With those two questions, the new Universal Apostolic Preferences (UAPs) of the Society of Jesus were introduced. The first one aims to show the path to God via the Spiritual Exercises and discernment. Why does this UAP come first?

It is a fundamental premise of the spiritual life of Christians that God maintains a continual dialogue with human beings and with history. Without that, nothing else would make sense. The Bible is a selection of examples of the very long story of God's communication with mankind in different contexts. If we define God through the word *love*, then the deepest form of communication is what love means. Those who love go beyond verbal communication and give of themselves fully. But for two-way communication to take place, a few basic conditions are required: God speaks to those who want to begin a dialogue with him. It is his desire to speak to us, and those words in the video introducing the Universal Apostolic Preferences are an invitation to listen. If you allow God to speak to you, you realise that he has something important to tell you.

God is the Word, as the prologue to the Gospel of John tells us. This can also be expressed through other words: let God love you because he is the one who attracts you. The Prophet Isaiah said that the Lord seduced him… and that he allowed himself to be seduced. This

Let God love you because he is the one who attracts you.

communication has a dimension beyond listening. It relates to feelings and affectivity. That is why the UAPs are essential for us. If we are not open to God speaking to us, there is no way forward. We find the meaning of life in the love of God, which turns into love for our neighbour. When God speaks to us, it is to tell us to love, to draw close to our neighbour, and to initiate a relational dynamic of loving and giving. When we enter a process of listening to the Lord, we discover the truth of that saying of Teresa of Avila that might seem utterly crazy: "Only God is enough."

The first UAP begins with the phrase "showing the way to God." How does the Society interpret this "showing" in our societies today?

Showing means making something available to people, which is quite different from imposing it upon them. It involves respecting the freedom of each person to choose or reject the path shown. This is nothing new: this has always been the way that the Lord has made his presence known since the beginning. In the Bible, we see that God communicates with human beings by revealing rather than imposing his presence on them. The Lord becomes present, he offers himself to us, but each individual is then free to accept or reject him. With Jesus, this becomes something even more radical. The Gospels give us a panorama of every conceivable way that God reveals himself to us through Christ. We chose the word *showing* in the UAPs because it suggests freedom, both that of other people to choose this path and also our own to teach freely what we are offering.

What is the greatest strength of the Spiritual Exercises and spiritual discernment?

They are a pedagogy in how to communicate with God from the deepest part of ourselves, our affections. They lead us into a dynamic of affective communication with the Lord. They take us by the hand to listen to him and enter the loving dialogue that he offers. The starting point of the Spiritual Exercises is as much that God wishes to communicate with us as that each person is free to communicate with him. Only by starting from a place of freedom can we enter relationship with him.

The Exercises also offer a pedagogy in spiritual discernment, by revealing how over time God moves within each of us. On his retreat, Ignatius reflected on how the Lord communicates by stirring our affections; Ignatius's reflection led to the development of a pedagogy to grasp and understand this way of communicating. That is what the Spiritual Exercises are. Their name is not a random choice. We exercise to be in shape. In this case, we are doing exercises in the Spirit so we can train in the process of accompaniment that helps us discern. Although some people say it is enough to do the Spiritual Exercises once in a lifetime, the tradition of the Society teaches us that it is worthwhile doing them every year and to keep up the practice of doing them regularly. Discernment requires a spiritual workout if we are to make decisions in freedom.

There is a danger, however, that the Spiritual Exercises might be hawked as a commercial product that is for sale. That can happen if the experience of God is stripped out and they become an end in themselves, or if it is thought that people can "save themselves" through doing them, or become someone of "spiritual stature." What the Spiritual Exercises really do is help you meet the true God and remain active in the service of others.

Why do so many people (Jesuits, other religious, lay people, clergy) do the Spiritual Exercises without it leading to a real change in their lives? What is the secret to them really changing people?

If the Exercises are just a one-off incident in your life rather than the beginning of an ongoing process, they will not lead to a real change. You might have a moving experience, but the Exercises will not take you any further than that if they do not reinforce or nourish a process of developing a spiritual lifestyle. In our last General Congregation, we addressed the question of why the Spiritual Exercises do not always spark the change that they should, even in Jesuits. I believe this situation reveals the fragility of our own spiritual lives.

We do not make enough use of the daily examen. This is a key tool in Ignatian spirituality. Ignatius's examen begins with a grateful recognition of God's presence in our lives so that we can then explore our response to this. If you learn how to continually apply that attitude of the examen to everything you do, then you probably will change. That is what Ignatius recommends. But this form of discernment in the spiritual life works only if you have begun an ongoing spiritual process, and the Exercises, prayer, or the Eucharist are not one-off instances in your life. If there is a process, then it is possible to grow into a way of life modeled on Jesus.

It was the reading of religious books during his convalescence after being wounded in Pamplona that changed Ignatius and led to his conversion. Do you believe that literature still has the same power to move us today, or are we now more influenced by other media such as videos?

Many things can help, although I'm of a generation for whom there is no substitute for reading. While there's no doubt that videos, films, or pictures have the power to move us, what is unique to reading is its power to completely grip you and get inside your head, which is what happened to Ignatius. Literature is essential in the Christian life, to the extent that the reading of the Word is central to our liturgical celebrations. And, although we often read the Bible, the experience is always different every time. I've been fortunate enough to read widely since I was a small child. My parents hardly allowed us to watch television, and we were always greatly encouraged to read. If I went out into the street without a book under my arm to turn to in idle moments, I felt like something was missing.

Where is the spark that triggers conversion most frequently found?

That spark can happen when you discover another person and who they truly are beneath the surface. That's conversion: when you abandon your assumptions or prejudices and see the person before you as they truly are. That discovery of difference enriches you and shows you something you didn't know before then, with both its good and bad points. That's when you discover suffering, joy, and also occasional emptiness.

In my case, the journeys I made as a young man throughout Venezuela and my experiences in the novitiate when for a time I worked alongside rural workers and in a factory were immensely significant. My eyes were opened to ways of living unfamiliar to me. I recall one particular experience in the countryside. A man had died, and during his funeral, his wife embarked on a very beautiful dialogue with the deceased. It was her way of saying goodbye to someone she had loved deeply. Witnessing that triggered a conversion process. The Jesuit universities in Latin America have Ignatian leadership programs that encourage their students to discover other social realities. A number of different factors can trigger conversion in us, including discovering who other people truly are, reading, or sharing our life with others.

Is it possible to talk about conversion and a path towards God in societies which regard being free of religion as something positive?

Part of the process of secularisation is about being set free from religion, understood here as a social convention or a way of imposing a vocabulary or identity that allows little space for individual freedom and faith. Christianity is not simply a religion: it is a religious faith because it leads to a personal relationship with God. If society helps sets you free from a religion that feels like a straitjacket, it can actually help you grow in faith. However, to have this openness to faith, it is important to be aware of the role the sacred plays in society. The Gospel shows us that Jesus was very "anti-religious" in the sense described above. He placed the human person above the law and had no time for empty and exclusive ritualism, and because of that, he was condemned to death. For Jesus, the heart of religion was the living God, the God of life and the communion of love among persons, with him, and towards the environment. He destroyed an image of God mixed up with power structures and oppression. Setting that kind of religion free was a step towards a genuine faith in God.

What would you say to those who believe in God and consider themselves Catholic but reject the Church?

First of all, I would listen to what they have to say, to understand how they arrived at that conclusion. That idea of holding onto God but parting ways with the Church probably comes from a personal experience that would be worth exploring. Based on that conversation, I'd share what it means to me to have an intimate relationship with Jesus and to belong to the Church. Faith in Christ leads you to reach out to others to share your faith with them and cannot be separated from belonging to the community, which is the Church. That does not mean you cannot be critical of the Church. Indeed, the saints themselves were, and suggested ways to improve her. The person who steps away from the Church is completely right to reject whatever has scandalised them. But what needs looking at is how they might move on from this experience in order to try and improve the Church, in order to ensure that their personal faith in God is complemented by belonging to a community based around the Eucharist.

How do you explain the success of New Age beliefs, alternative spiritualities, and sects?

People's thirst for faith is slaked in many different ways. It is another consequence of secularisation because these phenomena do not emerge in societies where there is one dominant religion. I am no expert on this area, but some of these beliefs are very individualistic and do not demand any commitment at all to your neighbour. Christianity, in contrast, when it is authentically lived out, brings you into communion with others, and into contact with things you don't like. It makes you open to other people's pain and problems.

Some intellectuals are suggesting that, thanks to technological development, mankind could become immortal. Is it possible for this reality to co-exist alongside the concept of God that has prevailed up until now?

Any form of immortality which, hypothetically, might be possible thanks to technological advances, would certainly be different from the eternal life spoken of by the Christian faith. Immortality means prolonging this life but does not consider a perspective beyond human life. The length of our lives is changing, as we have seen in the past few decades as life expectancy in some countries has shot up from 30 or 40 years old to more than 70, with consequent problems. What age might we live to with the immortality offered by technology? I'd love to regain the energy I had at the age of 20, but not the doubts nor the ignorance I also had then.

What is so interesting about the Christian faith is not that it offers us immortality but that it invites us to share in the life of God. It implies life in its fullness: we have our origin in God, and we end in him. In his book about Jesus, Benedict XVI is very enlightening on this point when he explains that the Resurrection is a step towards full participation in the life of God and that is why death is necessary. It is Easter, and without Easter this experience cannot be had. One dies to this life to reach the next. But in a way, we are also dying through the transformations we go through over the course of our lives. In his letters, St. John says we have passed from death to life, and that, as we adopt the way of life shown by Jesus, we enter into a new life. Death means going towards more love and having a greater share of the life of God. That is why we speak of Easter and not of immortality. This is about a gift, not the fruit of our scientific endeavours.

The lack of serenity and reflection in the contemporary world is obvious. Does this scenario offer the Church an opportunity to help people slow down and reflect on the important things in life?

The spiritual life as such cannot exist if it allows no room for peace. That is something we religious also experience: we are determined to do so many things that at times we do not leave enough room to go deeper in our relationship with God. Times of peace and prayer are necessary for us to examine the life we are leading and enjoy a joyful interiority. If not, we can end up doing too many things and not living. Little by little, this strips our life of meaning. Many vocational crises in the religious life are connected to this.

The Spiritual Exercises, which we talked about earlier, teach you to retain a certain discipline in order to preserve time for prayer. However, this is a problem for everyone. In the life of a couple, there needs to be time dedicated to their mutual affection, beyond the responsibilities. The same thing happens with professionals. I recall a great friend, a social activist, who became the head of a trade union but realised at that point he had lost control of his daily schedule and no longer had the time to do what he set out to do when he had chosen that direction in life.

Unamuno wrote in *El sentimiento trágico de la vida* (Tragic Sense of Life): "Act so that in your own judgement and in the judgement of others you may merit eternity, act so that you may become irreplaceable, act so that you may not merit death. Or perhaps thus: Act as if you were to die tomorrow, but to die in order to survive and be eternalised"[9] Should death give meaning to life?

Anyone involved in pastoral care in parishes is well aware that day-to-day the subject of death never goes away. People come to Churches during funerals and Masses for the dead and you can end up in tune with what they are going through. I once knew a Jesuit who said that he preached only during funerals because everyone present hung on his words, far more so more than during a normal Mass. When someone comes to a burial or funeral, they do so out of affection for the person they are saying goodbye to. During the first week of the Spiritual Exercises,

---

9 Tragic Sense of Life, M. de Unamuno. J. Crawford Flitch (translator). Publisher: e-artnow, April 24th, 2020.

St. Ignatius recommends that you imagine the moment of your death and think about how you would have liked to have lived. That helps you examine your life and change your present. The presence of that limitation which is death enables us to live with meaning and integrity. That phrase of Unamuno's is an invitation to conversion, to change our lives.

What role can popular religiosity play in spirituality, e.g., pilgrimages?

Popular religiosity is a richly symbolic form of spiritual life, whether expressed on the level of individuals or of groups. It makes powerful use of images. The great challenge popular religiosity entails is how to ensure that people actually experience what the activity they are involved in represents, as opposed to this just being about doing something together in a group. For example, some people who join a *cofradía* (penitential lay brotherhoods common to Spain and Latin America who process in public during Holy Week carrying sculptures representing the Passion of Christ) lose touch with the deep meaning of what is actually being represented. Popular religiosity enables people to connect very quickly to an experience of God, as I experienced in base communities in Latin America, and I know this happens in the religious experience of the poor in other continents. When these forms of popular religiosity exist, the atmosphere of liturgical celebrations is much richer and deeper. That is the challenge: ensuring that expressions of popular religiosity based on deep experiences of faith do not turn into empty rituals. Contexts need to be established that allow people to express their experience of the divine. This Pope, during his time as an auxiliary bishop of the Archdiocese of Buenos Aires, and later as the Archbishop, was in close contact with the faith of the working classes. He has broad experience of this kind of pastoral care.

Until the Second Vatican Council, the meaning of Evangelisation was very much connected with proselytising. It still is in the minds of some priests and believers. How can the Church avoid sliding into proselytism?

The tension between evangelism and proselytism has always existed because of the constant interplay between human liberty and a tendency to turn religion into a mechanism of power. There always has been a great deal of debate, at some times more than others, over whether human liberty or religious considerations should prevail, and this has led often to the mistaken idea that they are incompatible. The greatest debates in this regard have arisen—and still arise today—when the defenders of freedom try to cancel out the religious dimension of the human being or when religion tries to establish itself as an instrument of power. We need to be aware of both potential dangers.

With the UAPs, great care was taken to avoid these tensions. We need to show a way but never impose it, because a Christianity that is not freely chosen loses its meaning. Christianity has been imposed in various ways throughout history, and we can feel tempted to do this today. Evangelising is about an offer, sharing a joy. Love is not about imposition but attraction, an offer, patient waiting for an answer that is freely given.

Where do you observe the Church falling into the temptation to proselytise today?

This tension is apparent today in many debates on public policies, as much within the heart of the Church as outside it. It's easy to see in discussions surrounding issues such as euthanasia or abortion. This is where the Church, as part of society, has to join in these debates and communicate a pro-life position in clear, straightforward terms. Members of the Church can't give up their responsibility in public matters. However, as a Church, we should be aware that in contemporary society these issues evoke an enormous diversity of opinion. Mutual and deep listening and honest, committed dialogue should never be lacking. When both sides attack each other, it simply turns into a power struggle, and the pursuit of human welfare is forgotten and twisted into arguments that are merely ideological. If our societies are to be transformed into places of life and hope, then listening with the intent of finding the common good is essential.

What do you think about euthanasia?

I'm against it. My personal belief, which I share with the Church, is that every person should be supported until their life reaches its natural end. We need to explore why someone would choose euthanasia, how they might have ended up at the point where, in desperation, they lose any sense that their life has meaning. We have to be capable of supporting people through hard times, when they can't find any meaning in life and think of suicide. I have known Jesuits who were critically ill for years and were barely able to speak. It consoled me and brought me joy to see them: when you visited them in the infirmary, they would greet you with immense warmth. Even in the most desperate of situations, life still has meaning. As a Church we should be able to accompany people so that they can find meaning even in the most difficult of situations. However, a clear distinction must be made between euthanasia and the unnecessary prolongation of life through artificial means. Jesuits often decide that they wish to die in peace without artificial life support. This is a subject we have been reflecting upon since the time of Pope Pius XII, when these advances in medicine first began to develop. Death is a natural process, something quite different from euthanasia. *Samaritanus Bonus*, the letter from the Congregation of the Doctrine of Faith, is very enlightening on this subject. It goes much further than a simplistic rejection of euthanasia and recommends a path towards the holistic care of human life.

Do you support laws regulating euthanasia?

With regard to legislation, I think it is crucial to recognise that this discussion will begin in many countries and that some will even go so far as to approve a law permitting euthanasia. Independently of this, however, it's important to convey the reasons believers oppose euthanasia and foster the formation of individual consciences as *Gaudium et Spes* (16) invites us to do, so that believers can distinguish between what is legally permitted and what is morally reprehensible. The fact that something may be legal does not mean that a Catholic Christian should automatically consider it morally acceptable. One question I am mulling over at present is how we can satisfactorily express our values as a Church in a way that is open and easy to understand in contemporary culture. It's a challenge, but one we should accept with boldness.

What is your position on abortion?

I fully agree with the Church's view on abortion. It is certainly countercultural but also very necessary. Life must be respected from the first moment of conception until we take our last breath. Abortion makes no sense: it ends a life that should be welcomed and cared for. I think it is extremely important that the discussion about abortion not be reduced to a question of personal autonomy or even to merely a religious issue: abortion is above all a human and societal issue. If we are not vigilant about the holistic care of life in all its dimensions and all its phases, we will not build societies that welcome and respect human dignity. Without holistic care of life, we are trapped by a throwaway culture, as Pope Francis has said so insistently.

Many women who consider abortion do so not because they do not wish to be mothers but because they are in situations of deprivation, poverty, pressure, and social exclusion that make them despair because they lack the support necessary to bring a baby into the world. We must strive to make our societies places where new life is welcome and that work in collaboration to ensure the integral development of each member. In many areas of the world, the Church has committed to this. The fight for life goes beyond objections to abortion: it is about the welcome and integral development of every human being. It concerns the fight for a life of dignity for every human being.

Quoting Oscar Wilde, the Pope says that "there is no saint without a past nor sinner without a future."[10] What should our focus be to try and bring sinners towards God? Mercy?

That phrase relates to another idea the Pope often mentions: understanding life as a continual process of transformation, with ups and downs, times that are slow and plodding, and others that are steep learning curves. At the heart of this is the conviction that each of us can

Mercy is the highest expression of the radical love.

change, either for good or evil, that no one is pre-programmed nor is their fate predestined. The starting point is revealing that God is merciful. Experiencing mercy is the basis for improving ourselves because it is the expression of the love that forgives all. Only the one who loves, forgives. Mercy is the highest expression of the radical love through which the Lord relates to human beings.

Are the Beatitudes the most significant passage of the Bible in terms of understanding what God proposes to men?

Without doubt, they're important, but other Bible passages may also help us understand what the Lord is offering us, e.g., chapter 25 of the Gospel of Matthew, in which Jesus conveys, through a clear image of the final judgement, the heart of his message, what it entails, and where mercy will lead us.

What God proposes to a human being is not a doctrine, a theoretical principle, or a slogan but an experience. Reading

10 Pope Francis, General Audience, April 13th, 2016.
See: http://bit.ly/3j9JM5t.

the Scriptures is useful as a way of listening to the Beatitudes, for instance, but the real challenge of evangelisation is how to establish the right circumstances for us to actually experience what the Beatitudes advocate. It is not enough to understand what God is proposing to us. We need to experience it, feel it, and live it out.

How important is prayer to you? What do you think of the Pope's Worldwide Prayer Network, which is promoted by the Society of Jesus?

If what love basically needs is two-way communication, then a time of prayer is time you spend communicating in a particular, inimitable fashion. St. Ignatius defines prayer in a beautiful way by explaining in the Spiritual Exercises that it is like a friend speaking to another friend. The Christian life is based on sensing God, who communicates with us through prayer. Nothing can substitute for this and, without this conversation, there can be no discernment. The Church would not be able to make decisions without prayer or discernment.

That is why the Pope's Worldwide Prayer Network is so valuable. When it was founded with the name the Apostolate of Prayer, it was with the profound insight that problems will not be solved if we do not pray enough. We need to promote prayer, and this network does so with the intention of us all praying together as a Church around the Pope so that both we and the world can change. This initiative brings together many ideas: simplicity in prayer, promotion of prayer, and belonging to a large worldwide ecclesial community in which the Pope is the unifying bond.

The heart of the Christian message is indisputably optimistic, but perhaps it isn't always presented like this. Is more emphasis sometimes given to condemnation than to salvation?

The message we offer isn't always sufficiently optimistic. This is a distortion because Christianity is a happy message: the good news. If we don't experience this or present it like this, we're doing something wrong. Jesus was criticised for not condemning people and for welcoming figures like Zachaeus, the Samaritan woman, and the woman caught in adultery. As Christians we should emphasise the Good News and the opportunity to make the most of this message. When, in contrast, preaching emphasises condemnation, the Christian message is twisted. Jesus came to the world to save it, not to judge it. His message of liberation and healing prevailed, not condemnation. We need to be true to Jesus. If God does not condemn us, who are we to do so?

"Love, and do what you want." Is that celebrated phrase of St. Augustine of Hippo the key to trying to come close to God?

That phrase is a genius synthesis of the message of Jesus. St. Ignatius baulked at writing the Constitutions of the Society. He said that there was no need to do so if Jesuits were fully living out their charism, what he called the interior law of charity. When someone is inspired by charity, by love, they don't need a rulebook to tell them how to care for other people. That phrase of St. Augustine's entails a full commitment to the life of Jesus. Nothing is a greater commitment than love.

"LOVE CONSISTS IN INTERCHANGE BETWEEN THE TWO PARTIES" [*SE* 231]

When St. Ignatius invited Fr. Manuel Miona, his confessor in Alcala de Henares, to take the Spiritual Exercises, he said, "They are all the best that I have been able to think out, experience and understand in this life, both for helping somebody to make the most of themselves, as also for being able to bring advantage, help and profit to many others."[11] The invitation to "Show the way towards God through the Spiritual Exercises and discernment," as the UAPs suggests, is not the fruit of a merely strategic decision. It is born of an experience lived in depth and shared with many through which we gradually discover God's particular will for our lives, "in accordance to the talent entrusted to each one," as St. Ignatius said in the same letter. It is an expression of the life we have been given and an invitation to others to open their hearts to the Spirit. The Chilean Jesuit St. Alberto Hurtado used to say that "The Spirit is always blowing but you do not know where it comes from and where it is going (cf. Jn 3:8). It uses each person for its divine purposes but respects personal development within the construction of that great, communal work that is the Church. All of us render service on humanity's journey towards God: all have a role in building up the Church. The role of each of us in accordance with God's desires will be revealed in circumstances God places us in and the insight he gives us at every moment."[12] Discernment means journeying together to seek the particular way in which God desires us to reveal his presence throughout history. It is the mission that is sustained by the Principle and Foundation of our lives.

---

11 St. Ignatius of Loyola, Letter to Fr. Manuel Miona, 16th November, 1536, in *St. Ignatius of Loyola: Personal Writings* (Penguin Classics) Joseph Munitz (27 Jun. 1996).

12 St. Alberto Hurtado, *Unpublished writings*, Paris, November, 1947.

PRAYER POINTS

Preparatory prayer. Ask the Lord our God for the grace that my intentions, actions, and operations may be ordered purely to the service and praise of his divine Majesty [*Ex* 46; cf. *Ex* 23].

First preamble. History. Remember that Jesus calls all of us and desires all of us to be under his banner, the banner of the Cross.

Second preamble. Composition of Place. See in your imagination the places Jesus is calling us to today, whether to console us and give us life or to challenge us out of our comfort zones.

Grace to ask for. Lord, grant me the insight to discern the call you have for me today and help me to desire and choose only what will lead me to live according to your will.

BIBLE TEXTS

Ephesians 6:10–18 / Philippians 3:7–16 / 1 John 2:16–17

» How do you experience your relationship with the Lord? What helps you continue to be open to his voice? What difficulties or obstacles prevent you from experiencing prayer with constancy and gratuity?

» How open are you to God's will? Do you feel free to follow him to wherever he is leading you? Why? What do you need to advance in freedom? What questions do you feel called to discern?

» What are your deepest desires moving you towards? How much do they resemble the desires and dreams of Jesus for humanity? In which places and through which people do you particularly sense God's call to love and follow him?

Triple colloquy. To Our Lady that she may obtain for me the grace from her Son, to be open to his call. To the Son, that he may obtain from the Father for me the gift of discernment. To the Father, that he may grant me this. Finish with an Our Father and a Hail Mary. Do not forget to examine what you have experienced in this prayer time.

TIPS FOR SPIRITUAL CONVERSATION

For spiritual conversation that arises from personal prayer, the following steps from the general methodology of spiritual conversation are recommended (p. 268).

For spiritual conversation concerning an apostolic work, the following prayer points may be beneficial.

First preamble. History. Remember that Jesus calls us and desires all of us to be beneath his banner, the banner of his Cross.

Second preamble. Composition of place. See in the imagination all the places where Jesus is calling us today, either to console us and give us life or to challenge us in our comfort zones.

Grace to ask for. Lord, grant me the insight to discern the way you desire that we, as an apostolic work, should show the path towards you.

Bible texts. Ephesians 1:3–18 / John 1:35–42. What deeply creative ways have helped us to show the path towards God and encouraged others to find it? How can we make our place of mission a space of welcome and hope for those who are seeking God? How can we make the reasons for our apostolic choices explicit?

Triple colloquy. To Our Lady, that she may obtain for me the grace from her Son to be open to his call. To her Son that he may obtain for me from his Father the gift of discernment. To the Father that he may grant this to me.

Do not forget to examine what you have experienced during the prayer time. The fruits of prayer may be shared according to the general methodology for spiritual conversation.

In a Church in Meghalaya, Kohima (India)
Don Doll SJ—Creighton University

Gazing on the world from the perspective of those society neglects is a key call of the Gospel. The Society of Jesus tries to adopt this way of seeing, to listen to the cry of the poor, to support processes of change in a socio-economic system whose unjust structures cause poverty, deprivation, and discrimination to enable a life of dignity that is in harmony with the environment, and establishes international relations that acknowledge all individuals, peoples, and their cultures.

7 Walking Alongside the Poor, the World's Outcasts

Safet Zec
Boat polpytch, from the Exodus cycle of paintings (detail) 2017–2019
1100 x 340 cm, tempera on paper on canvas.
Photo: Francesco Allegretto

Why was it necessary for help for the poor and excluded to be one of the Universal Apostolic Preferences (UAPs) of the Society of Jesus? Have they not always been at the centre of your concerns as an institution?

What would have been very strange would be if they had *not* been included in the Preferences. A concern to walk alongside the most needy has always been central to our understanding of the life of religious. However, this is not something that can be taken for granted, neither does it happen spontaneously, because it means taking action in a voluntary and deliberate fashion. What this issue being included as one of our four Universal Apostolic Preferences tells us is that this is something we cannot neglect or far less forget. The Preferences are the fruit of a process of discernment and tell us what our priorities should be because it's impossible to do everything at once. The four elements raised by the UAP are non-negotiable, while how and when to tackle everything else is open to discussion.

Our service to the poor and how we walk alongside them has obviously evolved. It was always part of what we do, although after the Second Vatican Council our enduring relationship with the poor was emphasized, as was the need to work for social justice and denounce the causes of injustice. We need to be at the service of the disadvantaged so that they may be no longer be so, and we need to accompany processes of social transformation. This concerns freedom from poverty, a situation we cannot accept as appropriate for the human race. Following Jesus Christ implies a commitment to overcoming poverty, the condition to which most of the world's population is subject.

Which current forms of poverty and deprivation pose the greatest challenge to the Society of Jesus?

Poverty is not an accident, collateral damage, or an unintentional outcome but is caused by how social relationships are established. The Pope says this very clearly in the encyclical *Fratelli Tutti*. It happens as much on a small scale as in global relationships between nations: we have a political and socio-economic system that creates and maintains poverty and obstructs ways of overcoming it. This can be clearly seen with food. The world produces more food than its population requires, but millions of people go hungry. With education, another basic good, the same thing happens: a huge proportion of the world's population cannot access it. In the past 30 years, the economy has grown to a level unthinkable in the past, but inequality now is even more pronounced than ever before. Something is not working in this system: it is an unjust social structure that favours and maintains poverty. Post-conciliar Latin American theology spoke of the structure of sin because this system is not centred around the human being and his or her innate dignity as a child of God. On the contrary, other interests drive social and political processes. If it is not Christian to deny God, neither is it Christian to deny the majority of people a life that is truly human. The love of God is made manifest through fraternity, justice, and a life of dignity for all. If our social structures create just the opposite because this is not their priority, then that means they are structures of sin.

The love of God is made manifest through fraternity, justice, and a life of dignity for all.

What kind of work does the Society do with the poor?

Much of what we do is with the poor. This is clear in our social and educational activities. The schools in the Fe y Alegria (Faith and Joy) network or the Nativity or Cristo Rey (Christ the King) schools, for example, always engage people. The Society is increasingly sensitised to the fact that we do not work for the poor but with them.

We should not forget the existence of the communities of insertion either. Their number varies according to their location. Many exist in Africa, India, and Latin America, as well as in Europe, Asia, and North America. They are Jesuit communities that have a more frugal life than the norm, that are located in poor areas so that the community members can interact with local people. Today, the trend is to create relatively small communities who live in simple housing in poor areas.

Making the invisible visible is one dimension of the Society's social apostolate. That happens as much with individuals as with situations of injustice. It is obvious with refugees but is also true in regard to people on the streets, exploited rural workers, or children with no family. There are many situations that need to be made visible as the first step towards finding a solution.

Is the Jesuit Refugee Service (JRS) the Society's most visible method of walking alongside the poor and the deprived? What do you make of Arrupe's foresight in creating this service 40 years ago?

Father Arrupe's prophetic insight illustrates his exquisite sensitivity on a spiritual, human, and social level. He saw with clarity something few people perceived at the time as a social problem. Obviously, migration is nothing new, but the phenomenon that has been occurring since the end of the 20th century and up until today has the particular traits foreseen by Arrupe. I think he himself would be surprised now by that insight, which he received from the Spirit.

Initially the refugee service was set up to address a temporary issue, but as the years went by, it became apparent that this problem was not temporary—quite the opposite. Today, we see that the factors that cause poverty are also the same as those behind the phenomenon of refugees and migrants. Millions of people leave their country every year, not because they want to or out of curiosity but because this is the only way to save their lives and the lives of their families.

How did Arrupe end up founding the JRS?

The Jesuit Superior General has privileged access to a great deal of information and spends a great deal of time reading reports from the provinces and analyses of what is happening in places with a Jesuit presence. This is where the problems come out, so you build up a broad overall picture. Arrupe was particularly sensitive to this, having experienced the impact of the nuclear bomb in Hiroshima. When he came across the phenomenon of the boat people, refugees fleeing from Vietnam due to the war, he knew he had to help them. What was initially perceived as a crisis later emerged as a chronic global affliction. He wanted this problem to be understood, to be made visible, and for the people affected to receive care. Furthermore, he wanted the root cause of their problems to be examined head-on. Arrupe was the catalyst for meeting the concerns that already existed on the ground.

How many people does the JRS help today?

The JRS exists in 56 countries today and helps at least one out of every 100 displaced people or refugees in the world, i.e., it directly gives a helping hand to approximately 800,000 people every year. This is possible thanks to the huge numbers of people across the world who donate resources to different projects and to the administration who manage to get this help directly to the displaced and refugees. One of the first visits I made as Superior General was to Nairobi in Kenya, where I was impressed to find that the JRS there was offering education to refugees from South Sudan. Shortly afterwards, I went to Sri Lanka, where I attended the graduation of young people who had been educated thanks to the long-distance learning program offered by the JRS. It was wonderful to witness the joy of those boys and their families. Most had been destroyed by the war. There were practically only mothers present because the fathers had died in combat.

The care offered by the JRS has evolved a great deal. It now goes way beyond helping out when crisis strikes and supports the people affected by crisis by offering them educational alternatives, which very often they cannot access in the countries they have fled to. When there are no schools, the JRS offers programs of long-distance learning at all levels, including university studies, thanks to an agreement with various of the Societies' universities. They provide internet connections, technological equipment, and accompaniment, while the vocational education programs on offer aim to set the refugees up for life and enable them to find jobs.

Do refugees need greater visibility?

Yes, without a doubt. The poor are normally invisible to the vast majority of people. No one sees them except during a crisis. The same thing happens to migrants and refugees. That is why one of the key roles of the JRS is to make them visible and lobby for policies that support their integration into their host countries. Often prejudices and legal obstacles impede their access to health care, educational services, and the job market. That encourages the rise of illegal jobs, even slavery, which by facilitating human trafficking involves an additional form of exploitation. It is difficult to give real figures for this problem, but some analysts compare human trafficking to arms or drugs trafficking in terms of the sums of money involved. But we are talking here about human beings, not merchandise. This is unacceptable, something which cries out to Heaven. We need to dig into the underlying causes of this phenomenon.

Does the vow of poverty have a special meaning for the Jesuits, and does it mean they have a special link to the poor?

The vow of poverty is an expression of religious commitment, not only within the Society but in the life of all religious. It means choosing God's way of being, the way of Jesus in the Gospels. That is why Benedict XVI says that the preferential option for the poor is a Christological option and not primarily sociological. Within the Church, following Jesus has always been understood as being linked to poverty and the poor. The Jesuits live out this vow of poverty as a promise of inner freedom, as it allows us to be completely available for the mission. Without this interior freedom, it is impossible to be available to God, to discern or accept whatever new situation life may offer you.

The vow of poverty guarantees detachment from a given place, job, culture, lifestyle, language, or even good health. Attachment anchors you. It restricts your geographical freedom of movement. It removes your capacity for discernment. Poverty, on the contrary, allows you to detach from having an income, a given lifestyle, or resources to depend on. That does not mean we do not need resources, but it is one thing to use them and quite another to be attached to them. We need to abandon ourselves to God's hands and experience his mercy. That is the meaning of poverty in the Old Testament, which St. Teresa expressed so aptly with her phrase, "Only God is enough." Placing oneself in the hands of God may sound poetic, but what this means in practice is being in the hands of your brothers.

Isn't that rather nerve-wracking?

In a culture like ours it's certainly sometimes difficult. A Jesuit who, for instance, teaches in a university, will receive the same salary as a colleague who isn't part of the Society and who will keep his family on his earnings. In the case of the Jesuit, that money will go to the community because whatever he earns is for the community and its mission. Poverty in this case entails offering all your earning capacity to the mission. When you enter the Society, you have to change your expectations vis-a-vis your previous lifestyle. No one becomes a Jesuit to become rich but rather to give the best of what they have in the service of the Gospel. Living out the vow of poverty like this leads you, without doubt, to feel a connection with the poor.

Why are poverty and conversion the theme of the celebrations of the Ignatian Year?

We desire poverty, in the image of the poor and humble Jesus, to be the sign of conversion. Ignatius was distinguished, among other things during his lifetime, for his embrace of poverty and his service to the poor. He underwent an interior change that his companions later went through too. What we are aiming for in the Ignatian Year is for people to go through an inner transformation, and that as Jesuits we may attain greater inner freedom so as to grow in detachment, including from our traditions and history. Drawing on this detachment, we want to re-direct our own lives and missions in the light of the UAPs and under the guidance of the Spirit. That is how we seek to attain greater intimacy with Christ, greater closeness to the poor, and to the fight for social justice, to listen more attentively to the young, and to commit in a more significant fashion to the care of the environment. Poverty can help us to do this in a more radical way through detachment and the freedom of movement it allows for.

What in your opinion was the greatest benefit of St. Ignatius's decision to voluntarily embrace poverty?

How he institutionalised voluntary poverty within the Society. One thing is living out poverty, which in his case meant begging for alms and sharing what he received with others, but St. Ignatius went further still. He created the professed houses, which were not permitted to receive a fixed income or rent. When the Society's schools were established, a distinction was made and they were organised as foundations. It was thought that, while the Professed Houses could live only on what they obtained in alms, or donations, the schools would need a more stable and secure financial basis. That was a significant contribution by Ignatius because until then the life of religious could be sustained only by their work and the rental income from properties.

For Jesuits, a life of poverty means that they have to earn their daily bread. This remains the case today, and the communities survive on the income from their members. Each Jesuit contributes whatever he earns, which goes into a common pot to cover essential expenditures. The communities can't accumulate money, but the provinces can in order to pay for the formation of young Jesuits and the care of the elderly and infirm. Apostolic work is envisioned as something that should be financially self-sufficient.

What have you learnt from the poor? Has this had any effect on the way you personally live out your faith?

I have learnt so much from the poor and from their astounding generosity! Their capacity to give you what they have leaves you speechless. They are also generous with their time and in sharing their view of the world. When you share the life of the community in poor areas, living in deprived regions alongside fishermen or farmworkers, you learn to see the world with new eyes. The experience of living with them really changes you. You might imagine that the poor would be bitter because of what they lack. In fact, the exact opposite is true. Many live with immense joy, without letting themselves be overwhelmed by what they lack. I have always been in some way or other in contact with various kinds of poverty, and I have had the chance to develop warm personal friendships with farm workers or people in poor areas. This shakes up your faith. These people live out the faith with a depth and simplicity that all the theology of all the universities put together is unable to express. You learn from them to live by abandoning yourself into the hands of God and depending on him. And also how to confront death as something natural, which is just part of life. Obviously, the poor would like not to be poor, but they have a certain freedom with regard to their circumstances.

Some people criticise the Pope, saying that he endorses pauperism because he is supposedly hostile to wealth, and that he is using the poor to impose his idea of the Church on others. What would you say to these critics?

Pope Francis has a deep-rooted commitment to the poor, which comes from his spiritual experience and relationship with Christ. I would invite those who think he is heading in another direction to read the Gospels. Pauperism is an ideology, while what he is doing is coming from a place deep within him, as was true of St. Francis of Assisi. It is an experience that causes you to see life another way. When you see your situation through new eyes, with a fresh sensibility, a lot of things become comprehensible. This allows you, for example, to see the latest boatload of immigrants landing on Lesbos or Lampedusa not just in terms of numbers or as a legal problem, but to grasp that every single one has a backstory, that specific circumstances have led them to take this journey, risking their lives, their hopes, and everything they can bring the country they have come to.

Do you think that the Church became spiritually impoverished at a period when it was acquiring a great deal of Earthly power?
Sometimes people make superficial judgements that exaggerate, for example, the riches of the Vatican. Then you take a look at its budget and see that it is equivalent to that of a small university in the United States. It does us a world of good that all this is far more transparent today. Of course, there's a tension between our earthly and spiritual lives, and wealth can also be perceived as an attitude, a form of egotism, of not opting for the common good. Clearly a Church rich in Earthly power jeopardises her spiritual function. Ignatius said, very rightly, that "poverty is the wall of religion," by which he meant that poverty protects religious life and the Church from that search for power and recognition by providing both with the freedom to serve those who suffer the most and fostering a transformation of society's values. This is a tension that we all face. Having integrity in faith is very hard. It is not easy for anyone or for institutions, or for those in positions of leadership. Yet we should not forget that the Church cannot fulfil her mission without the means to do so. It would be naive to think she should not possess anything because she needs resources to live on and to carry out her mission. But in order to have integrity, you need to examine yourself constantly.

What did you feel when you heard Jorge Mario Bergoglio, then recently elected as Bishop of Rome, say that he wanted a "poor Church for the poor"? Is the Society of Jesus complying with his wishes?
What the Pope expressed with that phrase is something that has always been very deeply rooted in the spirituality of the

Church and the Society. This has been even more obviously the case after the Second Vatican Council. The idea of a poor Church at the service of the poor has been present for the past 50 years in the language of pastoral theology in Latin America. That phrase reveals the closeness of Francis to the Gospel, something he has demonstrated in many ways through his attitude of service.

Concern for the disadvantaged is a Gospel aspiration, as is revealed by the letters of St. Paul, which in feisty and polemical style, beg the Church not to forget the Lord's favourites, the poor. This is at the heart of the Christian message. Poverty is powerlessness, the opposite of power. Although in ecclesial language we speak of an omnipotent God, we should not really understand this through our usual understanding of power. It's the complete opposite. The power of God is love, which arises paradoxically not from imposition but from impotence, from solidarity with the weak. Love makes us vulnerable, just as God becomes vulnerable for us. Therein lies his power and ours. That is why Francis never stops talking about the tenderness of God.

Love makes us vulnerable, just as God becomes vulnerable for us. Therein lies his power and ours.

Do you think the Church hierarchy has taken to heart the pastoral and apostolic conversion advocated by Francis?

Yes and no. The message as such has landed, although there may be one or two who are playing the fool, pretending not to understand it. Quite another issue is how you behave once you have grasped the message. Many members of the hierarchy have sought to implement a serious change in their personal life and in their life as pastors. That is not only in response to what Francis is asking but is also in response to the Church's own spirituality. Others, in contrast, resist doing this. They may be good at listening but are interpreting the message on their own terms. Others who are reluctant are playing with time, thinking that this Pope won't be around forever. There are also those who use Francis's own language because they think that's the right thing to do now, but tomorrow they will do something else. In any case, I think his message has gone further than may be obvious. Perhaps I'm naively optimistic. Francis does not preach through fancy words, but through how he does things.

What do the poor ask of the Society of Jesus?

To be close to them. You grasp this when you look them in the eye, although the poor do not tend to be demanding. Their position makes them feel that they have no right to demand. That is moving. They like to be treated with consideration and to be in a fraternal relationship with you. A poor Church for the poor looks them straight in the eye and makes them feel at home. Building our Common Home does not just concern the environment. It is also about us being able to really live together like brothers, to be mutually enriched through our differences.

Can a conflict ever arise between the Society's work in favour of the poor and its work in some countries with the social and economic elite?

That tension is certainly there, although the Society's approach in its universities is always to try and open students' eyes to what the world looks like from the standpoint of the poor. We should not forget that there are also students who start their education in Fe y Alegria schools and who end up joining an elite. In fact, one of the tensions that education for the poor needs to resolve is how to ensure when this happens that the person concerned doesn't forget where they come from and remains firmly committed to the struggle for justice.

When the prophet Arrupe signed the famous *Letter from Rio* [de Janeiro] on social apostolates in 1968, he warned that there was a danger that by going down this road we would pay a price and lose the support of some people, even those who, up until then, had been connected to the Society. That is the cost of being faithful to our mission in the Church. Some people who had supported our work with great generosity stopped doing so after realising that we champion social and environmental issues. Some people in the economic elites do not agree with the Pope's analysis in *Laudato Si'* and in *Fratelli Tutti*, and do not want there to be a shift in the structures of power. The martyrs of social justice exemplify this tension.

Working for the poor and denouncing their conditions sometimes leads to political discussions. Does it worry you that Jesuits get into this arena? How does the Society try to avoid being identified with a particular political ideology?

Experiencing poverty from a perspective inspired by the Gospels is the best antidote to becoming ideologized. Ideology, which always ends up being a way to manipulate people, does not happen if Jesuits are committed to the life of the people and in particular to the poor, the victims of unjust social structures.

Of course, when you enter the social and political arena, there will be attempts to manipulate and label you, but you need to be clear about the source of your inspiration and remain true to it. Political commitment is one thing, ideological commitment, which can lead you to view reality from a single perspective lacking nuance to the point of justifying the unjustifiable and perceiving others as the enemy, is quite another. That is what happens with fundamentalism. Living out poverty as a religious can be the antidote to all that.

What does St. Oscar Arnulfo Romero, who was murdered in El Salvador in 1980 for denouncing the abuses suffered by the poor and fighting for justice, mean to you?

I was shocked by the murder of Romero, who had a reputation as a good man. Even when he said hard things, he did so gently. His death, while he was celebrating Mass at the altar, had neither rhyme nor reason. We were torn up. Even in death he was an Easter witness to Jesus. I remember visiting his house and being struck by its simplicity. It was quite small, like the house of the porter at the "little hospital" where he lived. It exemplified who he was: someone of great and radical integrity. What happened to him is shocking because he was murdered for having encountered the poor. For the same reason, Rutilio Grande, whose own death had sparked Romero's radical conversion, was murdered. Rutilio, his close friend, also had the heart of a shepherd devoted to his poor flock in the town of Aguilares in El Salvador. Romero knew of his goodness, his self-surrender, and his faith, which was not tied to any ideology. It was because of this that, for Grande's funeral Mass, as a gesture of radical protest, Romero cancelled all the Masses in the Archdiocese and invited all his priests to the cathedral instead.

Is the Jesuit Luis Espinal, who was murdered in Bolivia just two days before Romero as a result of his preferential option for the poor, also a martyr?

Espinal had a rather different character. He was a strong man who denounced in harsh terms what was happening around him. However, his death was not the result of his ideas but because of his witness as someone true to Jesus. Espinal was always a man of faith, although some would interpret him otherwise. For his witness as Christian and as a Jesuit, I would say that he too is a martyr. That is why they killed him, just as they killed Ellacuria and the other martyrs of the Central American University (UCA), with whom I had a lot of personal contact. Their deaths left us all speechless at the Gumilla Centre in Caracas. I can still remember perfectly how shocked we were when they gave us the news. When I think of them to this day, I get goosebumps. Their witness is close to my heart and is a source of personal inspiration. It gets me in touch with what it truly means to be a Christian and a Jesuit, how to give of oneself. In the spot where their corpses were left, Mr. Obdulio, the husband of Elba, the community cook, who was also killed alongside her daughter Celina, created a garden with a beautiful rose bush. Not long ago, they presented me with a small box containing the petals of those roses. I treasure it.

A few decades ago, young Jesuits stood out for their strong commitment to social justice. Is that still the case, or is there now a greater concern with spirituality or other areas of pastoral service?

There is a bit of everything. To get into the whole area of social justice, one needs to have a deep sense of spirituality. The people who have wrought the greatest transformation in the area of social justice are also those who most nurture spirituality. I don't believe there is a lack of sensitivity towards either domain today. Young Jesuits still retain a great concern for all areas of the apostolate: pastoral care, spirituality, being close to people and to the life of the poor. Perhaps there are fewer insertion communities choosing to live in deprived areas, but that is due to various reasons, some of a practical nature, and sometimes because our communities need to be more mixed in character.

"FRIENDSHIP WITH THE POOR MAKES US FRIENDS WITH THE ETERNAL KING"[13]

A few months ago, a Jesuit died suddenly in his bedroom. Although he was already advanced in years, his death was still a surprise. He had remained active with all the energy of a man driven on by the mission of Christ. As a Jesuit, he had important leadership roles and great influence at key moments in the history of some of the countries he was sent to on mission, due to the significance of the works he had founded and the social and ecclesial processes he had supported. The author of various books and a university professor, he built bridges and created networks. The news of his death spread rapidly via social media, and soon the Jesuits of his province began to receive messages of condolence. However, the messages did not highlight the important roles he had played nor his writing. Instead, they expressed gratitude for the integrity of his witness. He had lived for many years among the poor and was completely committed to their cause. He walked alongside them as his companions on his mission, and he had inspired many young people to commit to creating a more just and humane world. The most moving messages related to the memories of some of the poor people who had journeyed alongside him on the mission. "I imagine that X will be happy to meet with him in Heaven." "How I would love to see the embrace that he and Y exchange when they meet once again in the house of the Father." They echoed the words of the Bishop of São Félix do Araguaia in Brazil, the Claretian, Pedro Casaldáliga: "At the end of the journey they will ask me: 'Have you lived?' 'Have you loved?' And I, without saying a word, will open a heart filled with names." It is possible to walk alongside the poor, to be companions of those who have been wounded by this world, to be friends of those who come last. We have many witnesses of this.

---

13 St. Ignatius of Loyola, Letter to Doimo Nascio, August 10th, 1546, Letters of St. Ignatius of Loyola, selected and translated by William J. Young, SJ (Chicago: Loyola University Press, 1959).

PRAYER POINTS

Composition of place. Go in your imagination to places where you know there is deprivation and poverty. Look at the roads, the condition of the houses, etc.

Grace to ask for. Lord, help me to become a neighbour to the poor and excluded, to work with them and learn from them so that I may find you at the heart of the difficult situations in our wounded world.

First point. Recall your encounters with those who live in poverty: their faces, their words, their dreams and hopes. Reflect on them and draw spiritual profit from this.

Second point. Remember a time when you were welcomed with generosity and simplicity in the house of someone with few material resources. Reflect and draw spiritual profit from this.

BIBLE TEXTS

Mark 12:41–44 / Mark 11:5–27 / Luke 4:16–30

» Who are the poorest of the poor in your current surroundings? Do you know their names? Do you know their needs? What do you they reveal to you about God?

» What do situations of poverty, exclusion, and injustice in this world inspire you to do? What is God calling you to do in their midst?

» What kind of personal and community commitments is the Lord calling us to, regarding the hopes and dreams of the poorest of the poor? What forms of personal and community conversion do the new kinds of poverty in our world require of us?

Colloquy. Imagining Christ Our Lord is before me on the Cross, have a colloquy with him about how as Creator and Lord he has come to make himself poor for my sins. Have another, examining myself: what have I done for Christ? What am I doing for Christ, what should I do for Christ (cf. *Ex* 53). Finish with an Our Father and a Hail Mary. Do not forget to examine what has come up during the prayer time.

TIPS FOR SPIRITUAL CONVERSATION

For spiritual conversation that arises from personal prayer, the following steps from the general methodology of spiritual conversation are recommended (p. 268).

For spiritual conversation concerning an apostolic work, the following prayer points may be beneficial:

Composition of place. Recall the faces of people who live in poverty, deprivation, and exclusion near the apostolic work which you are part of.

Grace to ask for. Lord, may we listen to the cry of the poor and invite them to share our table.

Bible text. Mark 10:28–31: What place do the "last" have in our apostolic plans? What helps us to discover those who are "last" in our life and mission? How can we make our apostolic work a space of welcome and encouragement for the most disadvantaged in our world?

Colloquy. Imagining Christ Our Lord is before you, on the Cross, have a colloquy about how as Creator and Lord he came to make himself poor for my sins. Have another, examining yourself: What have I done for Christ, What am I doing for Christ, what should I be doing for Christ [cf. *Ex* 53]. Finish with an Our Father and a Hail Mary. Do not forget to examine what has come up during the prayer time. The fruits of the prayer time may be shared in accordance with the steps of general methodology for Spiritual Conversation.

One of the four special guidelines given by Pope Francis in 2019 to the Society of Jesus was to accompany young people in the creation of a hope-filled future. As Fr. Sosa explains in this chapter, every person is unique, has special gifts, a vocation, and can make a difference.

8 Accompanying Young People in the Creation of a Hope-Filled Future

Photo by Enrique Carrasco, SJ.

The third of the new Universal Apostolic Preferences advocate accompanying young people and the creation of open spaces in society and in the Church with them and for them. How is this being practically implemented?

It is not easy, but it is happening through some very different experiences, some of which are proving more successful than others. In educational settings, there are spaces that can be set aside for us to listen to young people. We are living through a time of deep change in human history, a change of era, in which the Pope has requested that, as well as educating young people, we may also learn with them and from them. Adults need to learn about the new anthropology of relationships that is coming in with this new era. We are facing the challenge of living through this change of era intentionally. Listening to young people is necessary if we are to go through this process with them. It is quite demanding. It requires a deep inner conversion. As far as Jesuits are genuine, with lives that are meaningful to us, and align with who we want to be, we will be equipped to show this to young people.

Are you listening to them? What have you learnt from them?

I listen above all to young Jesuits and more indirectly and less frequently to other young people. What I have learnt from them is that one has to detach from what one has been through, that one cannot deify one's own experience. Attachment and detachment are truly important. We all get attached to whatever it is that gives us certainty and a sense of security. That is how we avoid feeling doubt and feel we can carry on serenely. Adults are attached to how we experienced our youth, but we must learn to detach from this. Obviously, that experience is important and is part of who you are, but it is not the only way to live, and you cannot impose it on others. Things can change and improve, and that is what young people tell you in many different ways. They ask you to reach past your own convictions and see things from another perspective. What you've done and that way of working may be sound, but there are other ways of doing things. We must learn to live with that tension, although, I repeat, it is not easy.

Is the key to this education?

This is absolutely crucial if we are to avoid the other extreme and live according to fashion, altering the way we think to fit the latest trend. I was struck by the experience of the Homeboy Industries program in Los Angeles, which works with local people associated with gangs. These are young people who have had problems with the police, an addiction to drugs or other kinds of addiction. Some have even been to prison. The program offers them the chance to change their lives through work and, first of all, by treating them as the individuals they are. That is what attracts them and gets them to change their lives and let go of a dependence on gangs, which is something of an uphill struggle. This is something that asks you to go way further than you are used to.

Does the disinterest in religion exhibited by young people in Western cultures worry you? How is the Society of Jesus trying to tackle this phenomenon?

There's a great deal of discussion about this: there are courses, books, and seminars all trying to get a handle on this phenomenon. This is the situation we are in, and we should evaluate what's positive about it and try to respond to it. There are good aspects about this process of secularisation, such as going from a more sociological experience of religion to one that is more spiritual. In countries with a long-standing Christian tradition, at one point in time, national identity concerned religious affiliation. Obviously, the process of secularisation generates conflict, but in a secular society, the place of religion today is connected to people making a free choice. People no longer go to Mass because it's what people do or because of social pressure, but because they choose to do so, as the fruit of their personal faith experience. That's why, in a secularised society, we are called to encourage and support people who are searching, to present the Gospel and what it offers, to foster authentic experiences of faith, and help people make choices from a place of freedom. That is how Christian communities become more alive, when they consist of people who actually want to be there and grow together in the spiritual life, rather than being there only to look good socially.

The Society of Jesus has a wide range of youth movements. What do they have in common?

There are many highly creative and interesting Jesuit-led movements for young people, including Magis, which is held before each World Youth Day (WYD). It organises activities for 18- to 30-year-olds, with a focus on God walking with us and how we can find him in the day-to-day. The aim is to help young people learn how to be contemplatives in action. But whether on the larger or the smaller side, all our movements try to bring young people together with the aim of developing greater self-awareness, which happens when they relate to other people.

The youth movements connected to the Society try to bring boys and girls into contact with cultural diversity. We could say that they work for and with interculturality. Another trait common to all is that they help young people learn about their own socio-political context. That happens through volunteering and experiences of social integration, which furnish young people with a greater knowledge of reality and teach them how to interpret this. In the Magis groups, for example, before the World Youth Days begin, members spend a month in the place where the WYD is to take place so they can visit and live alongside people who live in the most deprived local areas.

Are there any other Jesuit youth movements that stand out?

The youth networks of Fe y Alegria, an initiative based on acknowledging and listening to young people. It is a youth movement that overcomes cultural, socio-economic, and geographical barriers so that borders are re-shaped as a place of encounter, personal growth, mutual enrichment, and social transformation. This creates an experience of global citizenship which, as a sign of reconciliation and the fight for justice, wants to speak out about the main problems facing humanity. It is one of those intercultural educational initiatives that accept as an enriching fact the cultural, social, and religious diversity of this world and enable people to think and act locally and globally without contradiction.

How do you rate the WYD? Each event lasts several days at a time. Are they of value to the Church after they end?

Magis was established so that WYD could become part of a continuing process rather than just being a single event. Some people have a great time at WYD, finding it a really good and moving experience, but it goes no further than that. Through its various youth movements, the Society of Jesus aims to go further by offering a program of spiritual development. As well as introducing young people to social realities, all our activities also teach them about prayer and offer them an encounter with the word of God. The bare minimum on offer is exposure to God, principally through the Spiritual Exercises. Spiritual discernment also has a key role. All these processes are adapted to the diversity of settings and the ages of the boys and girls and include a valuable inter-generational interchange, when older members of the group accompany the younger ones. They all end up being accompanied by others and being companions to others themselves.

How do the Society's programs help young people leave their comfort zones?

One of the loveliest of all experiences is what happens when you leave the safety of your family circle and your intellectual surroundings. It is healthy to explore the parts of the society you live in but perhaps know only from afar. That is what happens when you go from the country to the city, or vice versa. The first time I went to an indigenous area, I had no idea what it would be like because I had grown up in the city, in Caracas. I had to learn a new way of doing my daily routines. I do remember that we were welcomed there with immense generosity and hospitality. Those who apparently had the least offered us the most. It was a very enriching experience.

It was also interesting to see the indigenous and rural people when they came to the city. I think it fundamental to develop something like this, a way of educating through such encounters by creating a framework whereby these experiences become a source of learning, self-awareness, and growth in awareness of the world and God. Helping young people have these experiences is a form of accompaniment that promotes experiences of diversity, horizontal dialogue, and the development of a universal outlook. That is how to overcome the limitations of our individual experiences and lead people to ask questions about the role of the world, justice, and God in our lives.

How does the Society of Jesus accompany young people on their journey of discernment so they can find their vocation?

Accompaniment is intimately linked to Ignatian spirituality and pedagogy. It always includes an element of personalised care and attention for the individual, whether via a spiritual companion, a pastoral care worker, or teachers. The key thing is being there. But first of all, you need to be close to them. If you are not readily available, you can't be a companion. Then you have to give this time, something that adults in general and Jesuits in particular sometimes find hard because we tend to be caught up with various activities. With this, however,

> **The key thing is being there. But first of all you need to be close to them.**

you need to waste time, sometimes to chat about silly things, as that is the only way to create a space in which the big issues can come up later. You also need to have a huge amount of patience, not speak for the young person, and not try to hurry the process. The companion can usually see clearly, way before the young person they accompany, what the next step is, but should encourage them to figure this out for themselves.

In recent years, a number of internet initiatives have emerged that aim to evangelise young people, some of them led by Jesuits. What do you think of them?

With the development of the media and social media, many Jesuits have started up all kinds of digital evangelisation programs, ranging from ways of helping people pray systematically to offering the Spiritual Exercises online. We have also committed to evangelising via cultural outreach and dialogue on social media. The Apostolic body of the Society tries to use every possible method and means of evangelisation. Many of these initiatives stem from the creativity of their drivers. Vast numbers of all kinds of projects in the domain of spiritual accompaniment have been created during the pandemic. They provide virtual meeting places for young people, using methods and an approach they feel at home with. These initiatives from the Jesuits have been quite positive.

The youth work of the Society of Jesus includes working with non-Christians. Can you tell us a bit more about this?

Yes, this is about service and teamwork, and everyone who is involved in this finds it meaningful. Youth work cannot be limited to Christians, and it also evolves in settings where Christians are a minority. The objective, however, is always the same: to help young people know themselves and the reality they live in better. We show the path towards God, although it does not always lead to them becoming Christians. The important thing is that it leads to every individual converting to a deeper life, one filled with meaning.

Youth movements with a clear Christian identity also develop in secularised countries where there is great indifference to religion. That does not prevent very generous people volunteering or getting involved in social work. When Ignatius was wounded in Pamplona, he had to re-imagine his life. Before then, he had a small mission: he wanted to earn fame as a soldier. Gradually, he realised that life held greater prospects for him. He realised that God had a greater dream for him. That is the heart of Ignatian youth work: helping people jettison the small dreams they have for themselves and realise that there is a much bigger dream. Faith can help us do that and go beyond our own limited horizons.

Young people spend a great deal of time today on the internet, where they sometimes have a greater number of close friendships than they do in person. What do you think of social media?

The digital world offers everyone amazing opportunities. It is more than a tool; it is a means, a space, a dimension in which we must be present and that is typical of the anthropological change we are now going through. It goes way beyond how we behave or communicate. This is a process that is barely beginning, and no one knows how it will evolve. We can make the most of it to grow in freedom and the making of well-discerned decisions.

Of course, it also poses risks: it can reinforce a superficial approach to getting to know people. And, as my predecessor Adolfo Nicolás remarked, this is how we run the risk of having so many options that in the end we really end up having none. The same thing happens with people. We might know a lot of people, but those relationships might be superficial. It is easy to get distracted on social media. One runs the risk of missing out on the richness of personal relationships and not developing any ability to communicate offline. But we cannot ignore social media's enormous apostolic potential for evangelisation and the fact that this is where a huge number of young people today interact and chat.

How can we ensure that a fascination with new technology does not develop into an addiction?

Unfortunately, the problem of addiction is on the increase. St. Ignatius would say, "It is not knowing much, but realising and relishing things interiorly, that contents and satisfies the soul." Ignatius invites us to an in-depth examen not only of our ideas, but also our feelings, so that we can see where the path towards the fullness of human life is leading us and can identify and reject that which deceives us, entangles us, divides us, and takes away true joy.

This is just what spiritual discernment comprises. We have to accompany young people by helping them develop this capacity, which they already possess, so that amid so much information and so many distracting and tempting options, they can discern what is worthless and what is of real value, and zone in on what is essential. It is a reminder to not let oneself get distracted or swept up in superficialities, so that one may truly know oneself and others in depth. It's also possible to promote this on social media, in the digital world, and that's why we are there. We should not just be caught up in what's new but try to go deeper. Young people also reach the point where they consider this themselves.

You are not active on social media. Why is that? Do you lack the time? Or do you not trust social media?

I use the internet, email, Zoom, and WhatsApp daily, but I abstain completely from Facebook, Instagram, and Twitter. The profiles up there with my name are false. One of the biggest challenges I face in my role is how to use my time. My time is always in short supply, as is my energy. I have to learn to use both in the best way possible, to be true to who I want to be and fulfil the responsibility I have. I spend a lot of time in prayer, reflection, leisurely reading, and personal conversation with members of my team or other people. That is the only way I'm able to take properly discerned decisions. It's a rhythm quite different from that of social media.

What do you think of Blessed Carlo Acutis, who has been called the patron saint of the internet? What kind of example is he for young people?

He is a rather attractive personality, a young person who was not out of step with his time, his friends and relations, who allowed himself to be led by the Spirit and remained faithful to his instincts. It is worthy of note that he followed his inclinations within the world of young people, which is marred by bullying at school and peer pressure. Young people can find in

Carlo Acutis an inspiring example of someone who had a deep experience of God and let themselves be guided by the Spirit. Acutis developed his own personality, regardless of fashion. This actually helps us to be firm about what we are thinking of doing in life, and not get caught up in what others want us to do. To be happy, we really need to break free from peer group pressure.

In the Apostolic Exhortation Christus Vivit, *the Pope acknowledges that some young people feel that the presence of the Church is "a nuisance, even an irritant."[14] How can that perception be reversed? Do you think that is also how they see the Society of Jesus?*

We are part of the Church, so of course some people may also see us like this. We need to ask what the cause of their irritation is, if it comes from a misunderstanding, or from not being listened to and understood. Perhaps, with some people, we will never reach an understanding, but if the upset has arisen because as a Church we lack integrity, then yes, we are facing an open challenge. One of the positive effects of secularisation is that it opens up more forums for debate and discussion, thereby encouraging listening and an exchange of views. That is what the universities of the Society aim to do: they try to offer and value plurality. That sometimes generates debates and conflicts, but it does prepare young people for critical thinking and open dialogue.

---

14 Pope Francis, *Christus Vivit*, March 25th, 2019, n. 40.
   See: https://bit.ly/3aQUPhK.

Another thing many young people criticise the Church over is that they consider her unfriendly to homosexuals…

That depends on the context. The Church is not only the hierarchy but the whole People of God in all its tremendous variety. This is an area where we can make a lot of progress. The Church has doctrine and principles, which I share, but it is always seeking to share the faith in all kinds of situations. I have certainly known homosexual people who have lived out their faith authentically. The Gospel is extremely inspiring in this sense. Although it was relatively brief, the life of Jesus had an impact on every context. He came to save, not to condemn. The Church, understood as the People of God, is missionary. It does not judge or reject any human being.

If you are poor, a women, and uneducated, you are highly likely to suffer from deprivation. If youth is thrown into the mix, that makes your situation even more vulnerable. How are the Jesuits helping young people who are at the fringes of society?

The Pope emphasises in *Christus Vivit* that the majority of young people live in poverty. We want to listen to and accompany them so we can understand this situation and work with them to build a hope-filled future. We need to listen to the world of the young, in all its diversity, with all its problems, including poverty, exclusion, immigration, and ultimate rejection by society. We should not for-get that a large proportion of our educational networks are on the frontier

> **We need to listen to the world of the young, in all its diversity, with all its problems.**

zones of the world and work with vulnerable youths. With these young people, we also work to try and encourage hope amid many different places, cultures, and domains, as a contribution towards the formation of just men and women, true citizens of the world, who are able to generate dialogue and reconciliation between peoples and between us and our Common Home.

What other examples of the Society's work with young people in the margins stand out?

The Eucharistic Youth Movement (EYM), which is associated with the Pope's Worldwide Prayer Network, is very significant and well developed, above all in Africa. It is a way of attracting young people to prayer through the Eucharist and has an important apostolic dimension. Thanks to its simplicity, it has multiplied at parish level. The Pope's Worldwide Prayer Network, which operates in a grassroots setting, helps to foster a straightforward way of praying.

Young people are very concerned about the environment. How is the Society of Jesus responding to that concern? Could this be a potential meeting point between young people and the Church in more secularised societies?

The Society shares young people's concern for the environment, which cuts across all societies, whether religious or secularised. Traditional religions have a concept of the sacredness of nature, which the secular world is just discovering. This is changing its perspective. Concern for the environment is also shared across the generations. Young people, adults, and elderly people are all becoming aware that preserving the environment concerns us all. We are all teaching one another about this.

What do you think of Greta Thunberg? Do you agree with her complaint that adults have robbed young people of their dreams and future?

I only know her through the media and I find her insight remarkable. To use Ignatian language, it is an example of "no doubt and no room for doubt." I also applaud her decision to stand up and invite others to do the same. But I reject her idea that dreams can be stolen, because that is impossible. Whether we like it or not, young people will continue dreaming. Like so many other young people, Greta is a dreamer. She will remain one. Her idea of our house being in on fire and of us needing to quench the flames and re-build it, I understand as a protest from her generation to require other generations not to endanger their inheritance. She is completely right to say that we are hampering her future. By neglecting the goods we should steward, we are certainly not making it easy for young people to fulfill their dreams.

I favour an inter-generational alliance, as suggested by the UAPs concerning young people, so that together we can build a future filled with hope. But we must acknowledge that this involves a struggle replete with difficulties. It's not as straightforward as ordering a package over the internet which arrives on your doorstep.

How would you describe the identity of a young person immersed in Ignatian spirituality?

First of all, he or she is a person who encounters God and other people, whom they have gone out of their way to find. They are increasingly aware of the social, economic, and political context in which they live. They keep an eye on how this situation is evolving and as citizens feel a responsibility for matters of public concern. They are people who listen to the Spirit and are able to take well-discerned and considered decisions. And, last but not least, they understand that their life is about service to others.

What are the young men who are entering the Society of Jesus today like?

In general, they are very mature and capable, men of great generosity with long-term vision who have rejected other paths in life. But this situation varies according to geographical location, which is why we cannot offer a homogenous formation program for all Jesuits. We have to respond to the differing circumstances of the men who enter the Society. In any case, usually we are quite demanding with new entrants. The first question we ask is not how many are entering the society, but who they are. We are not as bothered about numbers as about individuals and whether they are able to adapt to the Jesuit style of life. In addition, we have an unusually long admission process. It is worth noting that the great majority of young people entering the order do not come from Jesuit institutions. That is a point worth reflecting upon in our examen as a body.

How do young Jesuits interpret Ignatian spirituality?

The young people who choose Ignatian spirituality today—in particular, young Jesuits—have a different take on it. First of all, they show a great interest in going into it more deeply. And this is happening at a much younger age than was the case in my youth. Then, no young Jesuit would have dared to give the Spiritual Exercises, but today young Jesuits are doing so with tremendous success, freedom, and creativity. They are inventing wonderful ways of doing this. That is a big change. In the past, there was one standard formula for giving the Exercises, while today there is a wide range of possibilities, adapted to suit individual circumstances. In addition, we have gone from an approach focused on preaching to one of accompaniment. A significant change has taken place that has led to vibrant expressions of spirituality, which are highly appropriate for a context featuring many working relationships with non-Jesuits. Young people are still attracted to Ignatian spirituality.

What message would you give to young people and novices who are thinking of becoming Jesuits?

A clear and simple one: don't be afraid to set out on the path you feel drawn to. It may be an unfamiliar path, with sharp bends and steep ups and downs, but the one who goes ahead of you is Jesus, and we know we journey in the company of Mary. That is why we are devoted to Our Lady of La Estrada. This is the path we travel together as a body, as part of the Church that is the People of God on the move. If anything encourages us not to be afraid, it should be the fact that we are journeying together as the People of God on this path, which in ecclesial language is called Synodality. I feel very inspired by St. John Paul II, who insisted repeatedly that we should not be afraid.

In many places, the Society of Jesus has a large number of elderly members. How can they come into contact with young people to pass on their wisdom to them, as the Pope repeatedly requests?

Many of those elderly Jesuits are still very active and take part in our youth movements. Mature Jesuits tend to be excellent spiritual companions, because they no longer have the worry of having so much to do. They have a different rhythm of life and tend to be more available to help. An area we wish to develop is enabling our communities to be more open and hospitable to young people, so that there can be an increase in the exchange of views, listening, dialogue, and mutual recognition. We already have some experience of this. In Venezuela, for instance, school-boys have to do a few hours of social work, and they have the option of doing so by visiting Jesuits who are in the infirmary. For the elderly, it is entertaining to talk to the boys, who ask the most incredible questions.

"THE WHOLE WORLD SHOULD BE ENKINDLED AND ENFLAMED BY THE HOLY SPIRIT"[15]

It was in the corridors, lecture halls, and rooms of the University of Paris and of the Collège Sainte-Barbe that the Society of Jesus was formed, arising from the restlessness of youthful spirits. The *Autobiography* tells us that Ignatius was intensely devoted to spiritual conversation and to giving the Exercises to some of these youths [AU 77]. It also tells us that "At this time he was in contact with Master Pierre Favre and Master Francis Xavier, whom he later won for the service of God by means of the Exercises" [AU 82]. This is illustrated in a painting in which Ignatius and Francis Xavier appear conversing while they stroll through the university corridors: hours and hours of encounters, conversations, questions, and searching through which God's desire for these young men gradually became obvious.

There were also controversies. Ignatius was accused of being "one who led students astray" [AU 78], due to the great transformation experienced by those who took the Exercises: they gave their goods to the poor, they begged in the streets of Paris, they cared for the sick in hospitals, and more scandalously still, they lost all interest in the prominent posts promised to them in their careers in the Church. Ignatius, inviting them to place themselves under the banner of the Cross [Ex 147], helped them to perceive a world far greater than their own ambition and calculations. He helped them glimpse a future of such magnitude that it contained God, the poor and the sick, where hope was not based on rank, career, or prestige but on being open to the Will of God.

---

15 St. Ignatius of Loyola, Letter to Doimo Nascio, August 10th, 1546, Letters of St. Ignatius of Loyola, selected and translated by William J. Young, SJ (Chicago: Loyola University Press, 1959).

PRAYER POINTS

Composition of place. Recall the faces of the many young people around me, who dream and doubt, who are creative and in need, etc.

Grace to ask for. Lord, grant me a heart that is willing to listen to the joys and sadnesses, rejoicing and hopes of young people and that I may be available to accompany them in whatever situation they find themselves.

First point. Recall the dreams and hopes of my youth. Reflect on them and draw spiritual profit.

Second point. Recall those people who embraced my concerns and supported my projects. Reflect on them and draw spiritual profit from this.

BIBLE TEXTS

1 Timothy 4:12–16 / 1 Kings 3:5–12 / Jeremiah 1:4–10

» How much are you truly willing to open your heart to young people, listening to their concerns, and walking alongside them? What fears or kinds of resistance come up within you? Which particular gifts could you offer them?

» What concerns you about the young people around you? What challenges do they face? What kind of help do they need to forge a future full of hope?

» What insights and graces have you received from God through young people? How have they helped you to be faithful to your particular vocation? What is God calling you to do through young people?

Colloquy. As one friend chats to another, talk to Jesus, who is "young among the young in order to be an example for the young and to consecrate them to the Lord" [St. Irenaeus. cf. *Christus Vivit*, 22]. Allow him to tell you of his desires for the young people of today. Finish with an Our Father and a Hail Mary. Do not forget to examine what has come up during the prayer time.

TIPS FOR SPIRITUAL CONVERSATION

For spiritual conversation that arises from personal prayer, the following steps from general methodology of spiritual conversation are recommended (p. 268).

For spiritual conversation concerning an apostolic work, the following prayer points may be beneficial.

Composition of place. Recall the faces of the many young people around me, who dream and doubt, who are creative and in need, etc.

Grace to ask for. Lord, grant me a heart willing to listen to the joys and sadnesses, rejoicing and hopes of young people and grant me the willingness to accompany them in whatever situation they may find themselves in.

Bible text. Luke 7:11–17. How can we encourage young people to let go of everything which is in the way of them living fully? How can we enable young people, with their concerns and challenges, to evangelise us and help us to dream of a more just and humane world? How open are we to accompanying young people in their processes and searching? What concerns rise within us when we are close to young people? What is the Lord calling us to on an apostolic level?

Colloquy. Like a friend chatting with another friend, talk to Jesus who is " young among the young in order to be an example for the young and to consecrate them to the Lord" [St. Irenaeus. cf. *Christus Vivit* 22]. Let him tell you of his desires for young people today. Finish with an Our Father and a Hail Mary. Do not forget to examine what has come up in the prayer time. The fruits of this prayer may be shared in accordance with the steps of the general methodology for Spiritual Conversation.

Care for our Common Home, although this has only recently been made explicit, is anchored in Ignatian Spirituality and the Jesuit tradition. This part of our mission involves a project to love and respect the house that we build and share together, and it requires all of us to undergo a deep conversion.

9 Growing in Awareness of Our Common Home

Be a Tree Banana. Jason Dy, SJ

Until a very few years ago, concern for the environment wasn't on the Church's agenda. The Society of Jesus as an institution did not have this issue at the top of its priority list either. So how did things evolve to the point where Care for our Common Home has become one of the four Universal Apostolic Preferences (UAP)?

It wasn't just the Church or the Society of Jesus. Concern for the environment is a relatively new development in our civilisation, which, until recently, did not seemingly put any brakes on so-called progress. We had been persuaded that enlightened modernity had what it took to drive forward unlimited economic growth. Ecological awareness still does not come readily in our society. A complex process needs to evolve to burst the bubble of optimism surrounding limitless growth sustained by my generation, and even more so by my father's. I feel like I'm part of this process of a change of perspective. I was very struck by a report published by the Club of Rome in 1972 that looked at limits on economic growth. I remember my father giving it to me and joining him in a few discussions on the subject. As in so many other areas, there were Jesuits very sensitized to this issue, who under-stood the need for this earlier on. In the second half of the 20th century, some began to research this field and offer university courses on ecology and limiting economic growth. In Venezuela, which is an oil-producing nation, we talked about crude oil being a non-renewable resource and considered what might happen when it ran out. The need then arose to have a strategy so that this non-renewable resource allowed us to develop other, renewable resources. That is where the expression "sowing oil" comes from.

Tell us about your personal conversion towards a greater aware-
ness of the need to care for the environment.

That Club of Rome report had a huge impact on me.
Initially, I associated the problem with the development of
renewable resources. In my first years in the Society of Jesus,
I worked on developing co-operatives for poor farm workers in
rural areas on the borders of Venezuela. The scale of soil erosion
in the region deeply shocked me. History books told me the area
was chock full of forest, but I found hardly any trees there while
the mountains, bit by bit, were falling down. My interest in this
issue grew by the day until I fully woke up to the extent of the
crisis. I remember, for instance, visiting Los Roques, a gorgeous
but very fragile coral archipelago off the coast of Caracas. The
locals survived by fishing for lobsters, but overfishing was finishing off the industry. Observing the situation in Venezuela
opened my eyes to the environmental emergency we're facing.

How did you live out the ecological conversion in the Society
of Jesus?

More than 50 years ago, when Fr. Arrupe founded the
Secretariat for Social Justice at General Congregation 32, the
link between social justice and the environment quickly became
apparent. It did not take long for the evidence to emerge. In
1995, GC34 put forward a recommendation to the General
Superior, who was then Fr. Kolvenbach, to study how the Society
might help in resolving the dilemma then emerging between
development and ecology. It was thought that Ignatian
Spirituality could provide the basis for a universal response, and
that our apostolates could make a specific contribution towards

this. We also looked at how this issue was affecting our way of life. The fact that CG34 approved this measure in 1995 shows that it had been discussed for some time beforehand. Both CG35 and CG36 introduced care for the environment as essential elements of our mission for justice and reconciliation. Being reconciled with God leads us to reconciliation with one another and with planet Earth. What was new during the discernment of the latest UAPs was the fact this issue is now a matter of urgency for humanity and for the Jesuits' life and mission. Either we act now or we put the human race in jeopardy. If we fail to understand that we need to change direction, then we're heading for a really undesirable outcome. That is why it seems to me not only common sense but necessary that this should be one of the four UAPs.

Either we act now or we put the human race in jeopardy.

How do Jesuit schools promote the protection of the environment? And what about the Society's youth movements?

The response will depend on the context. For instance, serious efforts are being made to build ecological schools. One example is a school that has already been built on the outskirts of Lima, a city where it barely ever rains. A Jesuit brother deeply committed to the idea has successfully created a kind of Eden there by making the most of the limited supplies of water. There are lots of other initiatives along the same lines. We need to investigate how to make the most of natural light, ventilation, and water in our facilities. Obviously, it is not the same thing to educate students in a school that takes these factors into account as it is to teach them in one that doesn't. We need to take decisions that lead to us having a different lifestyle.

Another initiative I want to highlight is the BGreen Festival of Ecological Cinema, now in its 10th year, and promoted by Educate Magis. It aims to raise young people's awareness of environmental problems through a video-making competition open to students between 13 and 21 years old in Jesuit schools across the world. The direction taken by Red Cloud Indian School in the United States is also very interesting. It is located in an indigenous reserve and has begun to host a weekly farmers' market as a way of connecting students to the food system and building healthier communities. Other schools could also benefit from this, because Red Cloud offers guidance and resources to any school that wants to start a farmers' market. There is also the Ignatian Ecology Movement, which promotes holistic ecology in different parts of Latin America, with a particular focus on the Amazon region. Fe y Alegría and Educate Magis also organize other initiatives.

What distinguishes the work of the Catholic Church in this field from the many other social organisations already involved in protecting the environment?

The difference lies not so much in the kind of action we take but in the source of that concern for ecology. With us, it's inspired by our experience of God, which leads us to proclaim his Kingdom and to understand that it cannot exist in conflict with nature. The Gospels say that love, justice, and peace are the hallmarks of the Kingdom. All three are present in nature. The difference, as I was saying, should come as much from the reasons that bring us to take specific actions as from their ultimate purpose. For the Society of Jesus, everything should lead us to Christ, which is why we see our mission for reconciliation and justice as utterly indispensable. Ensuring that all things are reconciled in Christ implies care for the environment.

In his encyclical Laudato Si', the Pope introduces the concept of "integral ecology," warning that "the analysis of environmental problems cannot be separated from the analysis of human, family, work-related, and urban contexts."[16] How is the Society of Jesus responding to this call?

For us, the starting point for achieving integral ecology is the quest for social justice and the promotion of human dignity and the value of every person as a child of God. What we find most shocking is poverty and the structural injustices that cause it, which necessarily tie in to the issue of environmental imbalance. There can be no social justice if the environment is treated unjustly.

The Pope emphasizes in his encyclical, as he has done on many other occasions, that this is not just an ecological crisis. What we are facing is a social and environmental crisis. Solutions to the ecological problem cannot be found if we don't solve social and political problems. We need to understand this issue as a complex reality in which the economy, human beings, affectivity, ecology, and politics are interdependent. We cannot solve the problem without taking a global approach to it.

---

16 Pope Francis, *Laudato Si'*, May 24th, 2015. No. 141. https://bit.ly/3tgQTx7.

*The Society of Jesus is responding in numerous places to the con-
sequences of the environmental crisis on the poorest, most vulnerable members of society. Which specific responses have struck
you the most?*

First of all, we need to be crystal clear about the fact that
to respond to this challenge we need to partner with many different people and institutions, and we must learn to consider
this a joint mission that goes way beyond one-off projects. Of
the Society's own initiatives, I'd like to highlight the Ecojesuit
network which, in different ways and places, is doing a great job
of facilitating reconciliation with God and the environment. It
champions global transformation, including care for the Earth
and the most vulnerable, and involves some of the Jesuits' social,
educational, and pastoral institutes. It also partners with other
Church organizations, the scientific community, and various
other entities.

Another significant initiative in Darjeeling, India, is working to address the root causes of the poverty and unemployment
that afflict rural populations, through educational and environmental programs, which aim to empower them and help them
care for our Common Home. Other outstanding projects are
happening in the Philippines and target the promotion of sus-
tainable development and social justice, and also in Paraguay,
where an ecological farm-school has been built. This is a lovely
initiative to save vegetation typical of the region and plant crops
that do not degrade the soil. There are also other initiatives that
focus on academic research.

The field of nature conservation is tremendously broad. What is the specific contribution of the Society of Jesus?

I don't think we can speak of a specific contribution beyond the understanding that this is a dimension that no Jesuit can ignore in his life and mission. Having said that, we are making many specific contributions in this field, ranging from the university professor who helps farm workers to improve their coffee crops in Central America to the Jesuit brother working alongside fishermen in the Philippines. So this really depends on the specific strengths of each individual and the context in which each community lives and works.

Then there's the process we are all called to of changing ourselves. It's hard for us to acknowledge this, but the Jesuits are still very far from being kind to the environment. Yes, there are certainly positive projects, hopes, and signs, but equally we participate in the wasting of energy, using fossil fuels and plastic... We could draw up a very long list of all our environmental wrongdoings. We need to transform our own lives and witness to doing so if we are to have a different relationship with the environment. That needs to be the starting point for including ecology as a dimension of our mission. The two things have to go together. If we change on the inside, it will free us up to bring environmental issues into our ministry, whether that takes the form of accompanying people through the Spiritual Exercises, organizing camps for young people, or teaching at university.

We need to transform our own lives if we are to have a different relationship with the environment.

For us, this inner change is founded on Christ. Without him, we are left foundering in a vacuum of empty words, in an ideology.

Nature, the environment, ecology, creation, and the Common Home are terms that are used almost interchangeably. Which seems the most fitting to you and why?

I didn't really want to get into a conceptual discussion, but I feel comfortable with the expression *environment*, as it indicates the complexity of this issue. No one lives in isolation, and we all depend on an environment that we continually create and transform. The term *environment* seems very inclusive and all-embracing to me. Although the word *Creation* is far richer and more resonant for us believers, personally I avoid using the word because it's a theological concept that many people cannot relate to. We are all part of the environment and should not put up barriers that exclude anybody else.

Then, there is the image of the *Common Home*, which I like very much. Pope Francis came up with this one and uses it frequently. The environment is our home. One gets fond of one's home and takes good care of it. When you add the word *common* to the idea of *home*, I like this even more because it emphasizes that the home is not just an isolated space where I'm the only one in charge. We always need to consider other people and create an atmosphere where everyone feels at home. Francis also uses the expression *social-environmental*, which deepens the meaning of the *Common Home* further by reminding us that humanity is also part of this home and does not merely dwell within her. Taking care of humanity, especially its most vulnerable and marginalized members, is a key part of caring for the Home.

Which aspect of the environmental crisis worries you the most?

Water. I think this is the most serious problem facing us today, although it is little spoken of. We hear warnings about global warming far more often, but it seems to me that the core problem is water. I remember that a few years ago the phrase "Water is life, don't waste it" was commonplace in Venezuela. That hits the nail on the head. It's impossible to live without water. At the end of the day, human beings are to a large extent made up of water. This issue is linked to our quality of life, our health, and other basic metrics. Accessing water is a basic thing, although all too often it is at risk of contamination from mining or heavy industry. Not to mention how we are contaminating the oceans with plastic.

Are you an optimist regarding the possibility of slowing down climate change, or do you fear an environmental holocaust?

I am neither a catastrophizer nor an optimist. In Christian theological terms, I see the situation with hope. I'm convinced that it's possible to establish a different relationship among ourselves, with the environment and the Lord. But if this hope is to be fulfilled, we need to make an effort. I link this to a key factor: citizen engagement. That's what politics should be about: seeking the common good. It is obvious that there is no greater common good than care for the environment. But political commitment needs to involve everyone, not just the few. As the ancient Greeks said, we should stop being "idiots" so we can become citizens able to understand that our individual well-being depends upon and is subordinate to the common good. Politics should recognize that the common good trumps the good of the individual. This is something the Pope tackles with great courage in the encyclical *Fratelli Tutti*, when he speaks of a better kind of politics, meaning a politics that manages to engage all of us in the search for the Common Good. When a person takes on the search for the common good of society and the planet in their day-to-day lives, they become a citizen. Political conversion is very important for everyone.

You grew up in Caracas, a big city, but since you were at school you have been in contact with the Amazon region and indigenous peoples. What have you learnt from that experience?

Part of the landmass of Venezuela is in the Amazon but it's fairly unknown. My first exposure to the region introduced me to its geography rather than really to the people living there. I remember a trip with my father to the Santo Ángel waterfall, and visits to the Guayana region of Venezuela where my uncle worked on an ambitious hydroelectric and industries project then under development in the area.

I learnt much more about the Amazon through the Society of Jesus, and in particular thanks to the Jesuit brother, José María Korta, who came to Venezuela to become the director of a vocational school and ended up fully adopting the indigenous lifestyle and going to live with a tribe in the Amazon. He got the whole province to see the question of the indigenous from a completely different angle. Korta founded the Indigenous University of Venezuela, which I visited on several occasions. I had some really significant experiences there. Brother Korta brought us face-to-face with the reality of the indigenous world, drawing us into his dream of making its peoples a key component of Venezuela's peoples and culture. Unlike other Latin American countries such as Mexico, Ecuador, or Bolivia, in Venezuela, the indigenous presence is small and peripheral. Korta's sensitivity to it very much helped us all. Now my relationship with the Amazon is less about visiting in person and more based on information and reflection thanks to the Jesuits who work in the region and in the Pan-Amazonian Ecclesial Network (REPAM). I do, however, visit the Amazon missions when I am travelling over there.

What in your opinion was the greatest contribution of the Amazon Synod, held in October 2019?

First of all, it put the spotlight on the subject of the Amazon region and ecological balance, and it brought the indigenous peoples centre stage. The Pope was spot on about this and above all to include them in the discussion on the environment in the Amazon, its resources, and biodiversity. That seems a major contribution to me, as was the consolidation of the Church network working in the region. More than a thousand dioceses, religious congregations, communities, and ecclesial movements are part of this. This is a joint mission, and the more people "plug in" to the network, the more efficient it will be.

The emphasis placed on the People of God, the fact that the Church is not only comprised of priests and nuns, was also highly significant. The bishops and male and female religious who took part in the Synodal Assembly agreed with the idea that we are all the Church and that we each have a specific mission to fulfil. The Synod also helped to raise consciousness of the fact that inculturation needs to be thoroughly embodied in evangelization in the

Amazon because, if it is to become incarnate in local cultures, the Word should be preached in ways that respect and acknowledge them. That doesn't always happen. The Synodal Assembly and REPAM tried to awaken a greater sensitivity towards the indigenous world and a culture of care for the environment.

Are there any climate change deniers in the Society of Jesus?

If there are, I don't know them. What I have observed though, is some reluctance regarding this issue. It is not easy to wake up to the fact that we have to change our lives. What's even more complicated is subsequently converting into action an awareness that we need to behave in new ways. We still have a long way to go. It's not so much that the problem is denied but rather that it's hard to change our daily habits and let go of the idea of unlimited development. It happens to all of us, especially those of us who are more advanced in years. The problem isn't ill will but the difficulty in adopting the new way of life that comes with taking on a different relationship with the environment.

What strikes you about the commitment of Jesuits who work to protect nature and the peoples who inhabit areas like the basin of the river Congo and other, equally at risk, lungs of the planet?

I would single out their desire to share with great generosity in the struggles of the people living in these regions. Quite a lot of Jesuits have also committed to studying in depth the problems and their root cause in these communities. The Society of Jesus's attempts to understand the roots of problems have led to this inspired ministry to protect the environment and try to change situations of injustice. The work of those involved in this is remarkable.

The Jesuits involved in protecting the environment also display immense personal integrity. They understand that the problem and the process of delving further into it changes them as individuals and communities. As well as the examples of this in the River Congo basin and other highly prized environmental areas under threat, we should not forget the work of the Society of Jesus in India, where problems related to an economic growth that neglects peoples and their cultures are on the increase. One example is mining, which jeopardizes the land and lives of rural villagers.

Personally, I was much struck by the story of the Spanish Jesuit Vicente Cañas, who was murdered in the Brazilian state of Mato Grosso in 1987 for defending the indigenous peoples. What does his story and that of other similar figures mean to Jesuits today?

Earlier, I mentioned J. M. Korta, who was not murdered but who also experienced a radical form of inculturation with the indigenous people. Vicente Cañas was a special person who completely immersed himself in the indigenous world. He lived with the Enawenê-Nawê in the state of Mato Grosso, in the Brazilian Amazon and fully adopted their way of life and customs. He defended the rights of the tribe against landowners and the forestry industry. His corpse, riddled with stab wounds, was found in an isolated hut 40 days after his death. J. M. Korta, whom I knew well, also became inculturated to the extent that he was re-named White Heron, *Ajishama*, in the indigenous tongue. The name was very fitting because he was the image of Don Quixote: a lanky man with very white skin who, when he walked, reminded me of the herons on the Venezuelan plains. These men gave of themselves with immense generosity. At the end of his life, Korta asked me (I was the provincial at the time) to let him go and dwell among the indigenous people until he died. It was a heartfelt request.

What message do the environmental martyrs have for us?

People like Vicente Cañas or José María Korta reach a point where they are able to see their whole lives from the perspective of the indigenous people. They were as pained by cultural and environmental attacks on the indigenous people as if they had happened to them personally. They did not give up their lives just at the moment of martyrdom. This was a process they had begun long beforehand. Their martyrdom was, in the literal sense of the phrase, the testimony of their lives.

Neither should we forget the large number of indigenous martyrs. The Jesuits working in this field are not alone. They become immersed in the indigenous peoples' deep sense of community. The concept of being a community is lived out in a radical way among most ethnic groups. Unfortunately, we lack a record of all the lay people who have given their lives in the defence of these communities. The first are the indigenous peoples themselves. They are anonymous and all too rarely acknowledged heroes who some governments simply try to get out of the way.

There is a close connection at times between protected natural spaces and places considered sacred by religions in general and by Catholics in particular. Are you attached to any particular places in nature in this way?

The caraqueños (the inhabitants of Caracas) live in the valley of Avila Hill, a 2,700-metre-high mountain. This is our horizon, an inspiring spot with pleasant views. To me, it's a special place. It was where we went on school outings while I was at the Colegio San Ignacio. The boldest among us even climbed up to the highest peak. I recall one of our group, Brother Izaguirre, a Jesuit who worked as a carpenter. On his day off he would go up the highest peak of the mountain at 5:00 a.m. and get back in time to breakfast with the community. Another place that means a lot to me is the sea. I've always felt very much at home there. I recall when I was a child often going to the beach near Caracas with my family. And, after becoming a Jesuit, many were the holidays I spent in the Society's house by the sea.

What about now that you are based in Rome as the General? Is there any particular are of natural beauty that you like to escape to?

I greatly enjoy visiting Falerna in Calabria in the South of Italy. I go to the house of some family friends which is 500 metres up a mountain. You can see the Stromboli volcano from there. The house is on an olive farm, and in 20 minutes you're at the beach. It is a phenomenal panorama for someone like me who isn't used to contemplating olive trees in harmony with a seaside landscape. The location of the farm means you can also enjoy wonderful sunsets and starlit nights.

"HOW GOD WORKS AND LABOURS FOR ME IN ALL THINGS CREATED" [EX 236]

There's a photograph that has done the rounds so often it has simply become just another facet of normalcy. It shows a person digging in a mountain of rubbish in the middle of one of the world's open landfills. These enormous rubbish tips are an open, suppurating wound on the planet, a persistent cancer sucking the life out of their surroundings. This harsh reality is the fruit of our hyper-consumer society, which is permanently dissatisfied and driven by an appetite for whatever is new, yet throws away anything that isn't bang on trend. What is broken and what is thrown away merge into one environmental-social crisis that can only be defeated by a deep process of conversion that leads us to greater environmental awareness and a sustained commitment to care for our Common Home.

For those who base their faith on Ignatian spirituality, commitment to the care of creation connects with key elements of the Contemplation to attain Love. This invites us to "look at how God dwells in his creatures" and to "consider how God works and labors for me in all created things" (Ex 235–236). This is a God who dwells, labors, and loves in the gerund, i.e., who is constant and dynamic, being active and generous throughout time. Conversion happens when we recognize that God does not stop giving of himself through his creation because, by recognizing his loving presence in all creatures, we can commit, through our respect and care for them all, to love and serve him (cf. Ex 233).

PRAYER POINTS

Composition of place. Dwell on the many goods you have received from creation.

Grace to ask for. Lord, may I recognize your gifts through creation and feel moved to commit to their care.

First point. Think of all the people who suffer from marginalization, poverty, and social exclusion and consider how the management of natural resources around them affects them. Reflect on this and draw spiritual profit from it.

Second point. Reflect on the different scenarios in the world: how some consume in excess, while others lack even the basics; how some contaminate, while others suffer the devastation of pollution on their land, and so on and so forth. Reflect on this and draw spiritual profit from it.

BIBLE TEXT

Daniel 3:57–82: "All the works of the Lord, bless the Lord."

» How do you experience the social and environmental challenges facing us today?

» Inspired by your faith and commitment to justice, which steps do you feel called to take to work towards the care of our Common Home?

» Whom do you feel called to partner with?

» What kind of reluctance to engage with this area comes up in you most often? What kind of help do you need to get beyond this?

Colloquy. Like a friend chatting with another friend, talk to God the Father, "Eternal Lord of all things," and ask him to help you see the reality of the environment through his gaze as the creator. End with an Our Father and a Hail Mary. Do not forget to examine what you have experienced through prayer.

TIPS FOR SPIRITUAL CONVERSATION

For spiritual conversation that arises from personal prayer, the following steps from the general methodology of spiritual conversation are recommended (p. 268).

For spiritual conversation concerning an apostolic work, the following prayer points may be beneficial.

Composition of place. Remember the many gifts you have received from creation.

Grace to ask for. Lord, may I acknowledge your gifts in creation and feel moved to commit to their care.

Bible text. Psalm 104 (103). Prayerfully read chapter 1 of *Laudato Si'*. How does praise for the Lord for his creation flourish through our apostolic works? Which specific social-environmental challenges urgently require our attention in our daily lives? What specific steps should we commit to in order to be witnesses to his love for creation?

Colloquy. Like a friend talking with another friend, speak to God the Father "Eternal Lord of all things," and ask him to help you see the truth about the environment through his gaze as creator. End with an Our Father and a Hail Mary. Do not forget to examine what you have experienced in the prayer time. The fruits of the prayer time may be shared according to the general methodology for Spiritual Conversation.

The Society of Jesus is responsible for more than 2,400 primary and secondary schools and around 200 universities and institutes of higher education on every continent. More than two million students belong to this worldwide educational network that gives them the message that a better future is possible and that we believe young people can create it.

10 Jesuit Education: A Source of Freedom and Hope

Young refugee from Myanmar in a JRS School, in Ranong, Thailand.
Don Doll, SJ – Creighton University

St. Ignatius intuitively grasped the cultural potential of education. He strove to obtain an education himself and to send Jesuits to universities. Is academic excellence still a hallmark of the members of the Society of Jesus?

I don't know if I would use the word excellence, but there's no doubt that that the formation offered to members is intellectually solid. We invest a great deal in the academic formation of our members, not out of concern to clock up academic titles but rather because it's necessary for the mission that the Society is called to fulfill in the Church and in the world. Our founders were highly educated: they all had doctorates from the best universities of their day. They never stopped seeking intellectual formation as part of their priestly lifestyle in order to drive the Society forward. That is what we call "enlightened ministry." It involves a tension between a deep spirituality that leads to complete trust in God, and developing whatever resources are available to us, in accordance with our intellectual, physical, and moral abilities. That tension is a fundamental part of our charism. The Society does not want to be absent from the processes of creating knowledge in the fields of theology, philosophy, and science. It would be failing to respond to its original charism if it did not maintain this fundamental tension, which allows it to serve the Church and the world in a singular way. That cannot happen without the solid academic formation that accompanies spiritual growth.

*I imagine that maintaining this high level of academic forma-
tion requires considerable financial resources?*

That's right. It is one of our main expenses. Funding is
decentralized in each of the Society's provinces. Each one must
obtain the funds needed to cover the intellectual formation of
those entering the Society. We're talking about twelve to fifteen
years of study. Provinces also have to take into account the cost
of permanent formation for all the members of the Apostolic
body. This ensures that they can adapt as necessary to new contexts and the changes happening around us.

*Initially, St. Ignatius did not want the Society to possess sta-
tionary assets like schools. What led to the current situation in
which the Jesuit presence in education is so strong?*

St. Ignatius foresaw that the Jesuits would need to be free
of ties in order to go on mission from place to place, which
was why he thought it best not to found schools. He agreed to
do so in the end for a practical reason: the need to form more
Jesuits. It was then that the value of education was recognized
as a component of apostolic activity. Wherever the Society has
a presence, an educational initiative, either of a formal or infor-
mal nature, will eventually be established. This may be seen, for
example, in our work with refugees, which initially focused on
offering them care during a temporary crisis. Gradually, however, it became clear that this was a long-term problem, which is
why we began to offer education to refugees who have no other
educational alternatives. The challenge we face here is ensuring
that we don't turn into an institution whose sole focus is education. We need to retain the apostolic meaning of educational

service and not lose the freedom to move around implicit in our missionary charism.

Should education teach people how to deal with problems or how to try to be happy?

My basic premise is that happiness is what human life means at its deepest level. God created us to be happy. Everything we try to do is directed towards finding the thing we call happiness and being in harmony with nature. Of course, it's impossible to attain happiness without learning to face and resolve problems. Happiness, as Jesus shows us in the Gospels, is not something abstract and friction free but is found through a process full of tension and conflict. You cannot be happy if you are unable to acknowledge conflicts and live with the tension they generate. If you associate happiness with an absence of problems, you will never be happy. Neither will you be happy if your focus is only on problem solving.

A good education includes learning how to handle tension and conflict as part of life and seeing both as opportunities for growth. Furthermore, it leads to us grasping that personal happiness is intimately connected with the happiness of the wider community. We cannot be happy in isolation. That is the framework within which Jesuit schools and colleges educate. That's why they also educate students to develop a sense of solidarity and responsible local and global citizenship, so that they may learn to actively engage in the life of their countries and the world, become sensitive to injustice, and commit to implementing the changes needed for a better, more just future.

Does this mean also claiming the right to fail?

Some problems can't be resolved, but we need to learn not to allow ourselves to be crushed by them. No situation repeats itself a second time exactly as it was the first time round, and one learns from what one has experienced. We need to ensure that failures do not isolate us or crush our creativity. If we fail, it's not the end of the world. We can always try again later, perhaps by taking a different approach.

Then there's the issue of learning to live in solidarity with others: we have to accept our own responsibilities, but we do not live alone. There are people who can help and advise us, or partner with us so we can get ahead. Education for children and young people can include this kind of help with resolving issues, whether their own, those of the community, or other peoples'. Fr. Arrupe put this so well when he said that we need to become people for and with others, so that they understand that one person cannot be happy if all of us are not happy, and especially those on the social margins.

Surveys show that the vast majority of people believe that having a good relationship and a family are essential to being happy. How can young people be taught to cultivate these relationships?

A relationship in a couple is not the first relationship we have and will work out only if it happens at a time in our lives when we are mature enough to handle it. A human being becomes fully alive if he or she establishes authentic relationships, stops focussing on his- or herself, and experiences love from a source outside themselves. It is love that brings you out of yourself and makes you fully human, because no one can be the source of that love alone. That evangelical message inspires the Society's educational program.

The family is the setting where this process begins, although sometimes it can cause problems that people carry with them for the rest of their lives. At other times people can end up completely absorbed by an attachment to their family, which prevents them from developing other relationships. Maturity in these basic relationships makes it possible for a relationship as a couple to help people attain happiness.

What can help young people develop maturity?

Leaving their family setting is necessary. And that's where school comes in as a space that allows for a widening of your circle of personal relationships. It is a privileged place where young people can develop friendships, with their peers and perhaps some teachers, with whom a lovely connection can develop. Young people spend years at school: it's an important part of their maturation process and a place to build friendships outside the family. For many people, going to school is the first time they relate to people outside their family, and while there they learn to grow in respect for diversity and to value their own identity. As mentioned earlier, this is about learning to be people with and for others.

University, on the other hand, is a space that is much broader and more boisterous with a greater intergenerational mix. It is a bit like going out to sea emotion-wise and finding that you need the skills to navigate more complex relational waters. Another element of maturation comes from beginning to feel part of society, accepting one's own responsibility for the common good and therefore, making decisions not just out of self-interest but taking into account the best interests of the community. That is where the question of care for our Common Home, for creating just social structures and an improved commitment to equality, come into play.

How can individualism be countered?

Individualism runs counter to the Christian vision of life. The message of the Gospel is not individualistic. It goes beyond individualism by suggesting that we reach out beyond ourselves and relate to other human beings, to God, and to nature. This involves the very foundation of our life as a society. What do you base it on? A form of individualism akin to autism, with the idea of society being merely a composite of individuals? Or on the idea that what makes us truly human is living in society and seeking the common good, including being in harmony with nature?

It is easy to slide from individualism into egotism, which is the opposite of love and therefore the cause of conflicts and wars. The proclamation of the Good News of Jesus is a perpetual invitation to set ourselves free from individualism so that we can understand that we are all brothers and sisters.

What defines the identity of a Jesuit educational establishment?

We define the results we hope to obtain from them as the four 'C's: Conscience, Competence, Compassion, and Commitment. Conscience develops when a student knows themselves and the reality around them. They then become a free person who cannot be manipulated and who is capable of making their own decisions. Next comes competence. A student needs to learn the skills necessary to find their place in the world and be a good professional. Compassion is the opposite of isolation and develops when students are in tune with reality and understand the history that has led to current developments. Then, they are no longer indifferent to what happens around them. That is where the fourth 'C' commitment comes in. Students are not content to be passive but seek to change reality through how they live. Not because they see themselves as superheroes but because they decide to do something in a systematic way to improve things.

I suggested a fifth 'C', Coherence, at the International Congress of Jesuit Education Delegates held in Rio de Janeiro in 2017. This is vital if the other four 'C's are to be in harmony. That congress was key: representatives from all the Jesuit schools in the world met up and agreed consensually on a five-year action plan to roll out in Jesuit educational centers. Then, in 2019, we published *A Living Tradition*, a paper that helped us define what is expected of a Jesuit educational center today. This paper outlines 10 global markers of what is expected of a school inspired by Ignatian pedagogy. But above all, it invites us to enter a process of ongoing discernment so that our education can respond to changing times and always be up to handling new challenges.

How can this Ignatian identity be ensured when in many schools now there are very few Jesuits?

In terms of numbers, the presence of Jesuits in general is indeed low. Therefore, what's needed is for the whole staff in a Jesuit school to identify with what a Jesuit education is and offers. This process of adopting a Jesuit identity doesn't happen overnight. That means that every Jesuit education center faces the challenge of how to offer to their entire staff the opportunity for formation in this.

In this context, we have had some successful experiences and others less so. We've been learning as we go along. One factor has been a decrease in the numbers of Jesuits who teach. Another new factor is that we are offering education now in settings where Christianity is not the majority religion of the local people, either due to secularization or because our schools are in places where Catholics are a minority, as is the case in large parts of Asia or Africa. In this process, we have been developing various alternatives, such as school networks that can offer formation programs about our identity. Many non-Jesuit educators really want to commit to being apostolic companions who identify fully with the mission, and they carry out their work with creativity and selflessness in order to continue offering a truly Ignatian education.

It might sound paradoxical but a lot of schools with very few Jesuits have, thanks to these kinds of formation programs, a strongly Ignatian identity. Programs designed to gradually help school staff to identify with Jesuit education and to become authentic companions on the mission have worked well in Spain and other European countries, as well as in the United States, Latin America, Asia, and Africa.

How should teachers acquire this Ignatian identity?

By starting their own process of maturation. If we educators do not have the capacity to mature, heal our own wounds, and grow in every area of human life, then we cannot offer an education along those lines. It is still true that the best way of educating is through personal testimony. The conversion of teachers must go hand in hand with them acquiring the inner freedom that allows them to fully live out their vocation. If you choose teaching as a profession, you cannot view it as just a way to earn a salary to live on. Choosing teaching as a profession means seeing yourself as someone who accompanies students as they mature. That is why discernment is key.

However, ensuring that our schools have a clear identity is certainly a challenge for us. When a new teacher or other staff member joins a school, the school tries to ensure that they understand and share its identity, even if they do not profess the Catholic faith. Sharing a common identity is key to what the school and its way of teaching offers. Whoever agrees and freely chooses to work in a Jesuit school commits to respecting its core values and supporting its efforts to truly live out the mission of the Society of Jesus.

What does conversion in schools mean to you? Does it involve embracing Catholicism?

What is sought is a conversion to the Society's educational mission, which is not necessarily linked to religious faith. Our aim is for teachers to know and identify with our mission and identity. We offer students an opportunity for personal conversion guided by the aforementioned four 'Cs'.

Drawing on our identity, we present the Gospel of Jesus to students, as we are convinced that it leads to living a life that is fully human. We also offer them Ignatian Spirituality as a way of Christian living. Offering something is not the same as imposing it, and no one is forced to convert to Catholicism. Authentic conversion is only born of a personal experience that leads the person in question to make a free choice with regard to faith.

The Society lives and works in a variety of settings. In January 2020, for instance, I was in one of our schools in Nepal, where none of the students are Catholic. The school's primary aim is not that all the students should convert to Catholicism, but rather that they should become good people, able to help others and committed to the search for the Common Good. If any of them subsequently chooses to become a Christian, of course we'd be very happy about this.

How is Jesus presented in this kind of educational setting?

In the case of Nepal and other countries where we are present and where Christianity is not the main religion, there is a general sensitivity towards religion, which means that we can talk about Jesus without sparking the kind of initial rejection that can happen in some places that are in the throes of secularization. Missionaries should have the knack of tuning in to whichever culture they are in, so that they're able to offer an experience of Jesus that transforms people's lives.

In 2019, I joined an Easter liturgy in a parish in Douala, Cameroon, at which 160 adults were baptised. As I said, we're delighted to receive people into the Church, but that is not the sole purpose of the schools. The Church educates as part of her evangelizing mission. When the Church began to do this, there was no public education system and only the privileged few could be educated at court, in seminaries, or in monasteries. There are still areas of the world where the Church's schools are the only ones offering the chance for an education to whole swathes of the population. In other societies, in contrast, the state system is fairly well developed, which is why the purpose of a Catholic school in such places is to offer an education in line with Gospel values and to help enrich society from that perspective.

Jesuit schools include the Fe y Alegría [Faith and Joy] educational network, which seek to advance education for the poor and marginalized. Why do you think this initiative emerged in your own country, Venezuela, in 1955?

At that time, Venezuelan society was going through a phase of modernization, thanks to its oil revenues. Many people left the countryside and went to the cities. The State was able to offer incentives that were not an option elsewhere, but it lacked the means to guarantee education for every child.

That was the context in which some Jesuits at the new Andrés Bello Catholic University became sensitised to the situation. When they began to hang out with some of their students in the poor districts of Caracas, they observed the lack of educational opportunities for children. That awareness was then matched by the generosity of ordinary people. A bricklayer called Abrahán Reyes was just finishing building his house in a district of Caracas when he offered it as a school to the Jesuits if they could commit to funding it. One of the first students was Patricia, Abrahán's wife, and she learnt to read there. It was a process of listening, of dialogue, and of responding to specific needs.

Did the Fe y Alegría network, which today comprises more than 1,600 schools in 22 countries, develop from that first school?

That is how it started. Awareness of how much education could make a difference grew, along with a desire to be part of the process. Fe y Alegría schools began to multiply, thanks to a combination of opportunities, people's sensitivity to the issue, and their generosity. At first, it was only about schools, but very soon it became clear that other needs required a response too. That is why it is called the Movement of Popular Education: built into its curriculum are the expectations of a people who live in a situation of structural injustice.

This is an education not only intended to foster people's personal growth but to contribute as well towards the transformation of society. Put it like this: this is education with political vision. Education for the people does not involve them receiving a share of the breadcrumbs of the privileged, nor is it an instrument of ideological manipulation. **Education for the poor cannot mean a poor-quality education.** Fe y Alegría seeks to offer a good-quality education from the standpoint of people's concern to attain the social justice that will bring every human being a life of dignity.

What other kinds of popular education has the Society developed?

The United States, to give another example, has the Nativity and Cristo Rey schools, which are basically aimed at people excluded from mainstream society. These educational models were started by the Society, but today many others have developed them into a real work of the Church.

Nativity Schools offer quality primary school education for those who otherwise would have no access to this. They allow students to then continue their schooling in institutions of recognized educational quality in a system as competitive as that of the United States. Nativity Schools develop programs for school support and offer remedial programs, extra hours of teaching, and personal attention to each student. That is how they manage to help so many children. The quality of these schools has received various kinds of acknowledgment.

Meanwhile, Cristo Rey schools are centers of secondary education that, in an ingenious fashion, include in their curriculum opportunities for students to work in businesses. This corporate work-study program gives the schools a source of funding while also opening a future to students who otherwise have no other way to access quality education. This educational model has also obtained a great deal of recognition and has expanded, amid a great deal of enthusiasm.

In India, a widespread movement of people's schools for marginalized communities such as the Dalits, who belong to what is regarded as the lowest social caste, also exist, above all in rural regions. These schools also have halls of residences for students who come from far away or whose family homes are not suitable places for study. In some African countries, the Fe y Alegría network has been established and is creating opportunities in areas where there are no educational facilities.

Why not place all these people's schools under the umbrella of the Fe y Alegría network?

One direction we wish to pursue in our educational apostolate is the creation of networks, something which begins with the development of a shared sense of identity and solidarity. Helping each other out more and learning from each other is a very real possibility. That was something I witnessed very clearly in 2019 when I went straight from visiting the Democratic Republic of the Congo to Poland. In Kinshasa, I went to a school where the students proudly showed me their science laboratory. When I saw it, I was shocked, because the location was very insecure and it had few resources. I went straight from there to Poland, where, following the fall of Communism, the economy is booming and new schools are opening. I was impressed by the laboratory at the Polish Jesuit school and realized the impact it would have if they were able to share their resources with the laboratory in Kinshasa. That is the idea we wish to develop: not only should we work on developing a mutual pedagogical identity, but we should also look at putting true solidarity into practice, which would include sharing our resources.

The Society of Jesus has more than 200 university-level institutions that impact the lives of more than half a million students. Many of these institutions enjoy international prestige and educate the social and economic elite. What are the Jesuits seeking through their presence in these universities?

We should not forget there are also Fe y Alegría students who later make it into these universities. Through them, we are present in a socially diverse society. They enable our mission to be accessible to everyone. We want to make the Gospel present and help to make the Word of Jesus historical truth as much in the Fe y Alegría schools as in universities that have high financial criteria. Obviously, it is quite a different thing doing this in a poor area and in a university like Georgetown. Some of these institutions were founded to form Jesuits but later began to open up after realising that they could be a channel of evangelisation for others.

University is an exciting place that mirrors the complexity of society. In universities, one is confronted by many different ideas. The aim is to create knowledge, discuss ideas, and think about the future. The Society of Jesus cannot cease to be a presence in this arena. As Arrupe said: "We are committed to educating any class of person, without distinction. It cannot be otherwise, because the educational apostolate (just as every other apostolate of the Society) bears the indelible Ignatian imprint of universality."[17]

> **University is an exciting place that mirrors the complexity of society.**

Are young people taught in these schools how to manage success? And to accept the responsibility towards others that success entails?

If schools offer people a way of life, then universities do so even more. The challenge for the Society's universities is to open students' eyes to the complexity of social relationships in the world they live in, but often do not know, so that they may commit to transforming society in terms of social justice and reconciliation.

---

17 P. Arrupe, *Our Secondary Schools, Today and Tomorrow*, September 10th, 1980, n. 7.

That is what we are aiming for, but challenges do come up. For example, vocational schools provide a workforce for businesses whose identity is sometimes at odds with the identity we wish to promote. In the Society's University network (International Association of Jesuit Universities—IAJU) a working group is studying what it means to be a business school today, and the implications of making such schools instruments of social transformation.

Obviously, we can't guarantee that everyone who studies at a Jesuit university will adopt this identity. Fr. Kolvenbach, the Superior General of the Society from 1983 until 2008, observed that to truly evaluate a Jesuit university, we would need to look at whether its former students have become agents of social change and become responsible for the Common Good. That is the challenge!

The Great Gatsby begins with a memorable phrase that the main character recalls his father saying to him: "Whenever you feel like criticizing anyone, he told me, just remember that all the people in this world haven't had the advantages that you've had."[18] *Are young people being taught enough not to slide into the kind of gratuitous and devastating criticism so often criticized by the Pope?*

Friendship includes criticism, but not destructive criticism, which tries to crush another person because we don't see him or her as being part of who we are. At the moment, schools are facing a challenging problem with bullying, which also causes

---

18 *The Great Gatsby,* by F. Scott Fitzgerald. Wordsworth Editions (5 May 1992).

huge pressure for young people via social media. Its use raises complex problems that are not resolved simply by switching off electronic devices. We can't use reward and punishment as the basis for teaching. We see education as a way of accompanying our students so that every teenager can be helped as an individual to find their own way to withstand bullying and avoid becoming a bully. That is one of the greatest challenges of education today. The use of social media is increasing quickly, and it deploys code words that educator-companions are not always able to grasp in time.

Another key issue is forming critical minds capable of learning how to learn. Some kinds of skills may end up being irrelevant in the near future. Forming young people in critical thinking prevents their getting stuck with the beliefs they acquired at age 10 or 15 and enables them to interact with the society, mentalities, and institutions of their time. Authentic critical thinking leads to transformative action and continual improvement.

Should vocations to the mission be taught in the schools?

You can't learn the mission, only receive it. It isn't homework or a job on a to-do list. It is a way of understanding the meaning of life. It is received through a call, which, of course, you have to listen to and choose to follow. That is where discernment really comes into play: it facilitates the process through which you hear the call and decide or refuse to follow it. That is the process we try to promote in our schools and spirituality centers. It is normal for young people to ask questions about the meaning of life. This is the time in your life when you decide where to focus your energies and skills. We want to accompany young people through this stage of their lives. The journey that led to the Youth Synod and in the Synodal Assembly itself made it quite clear that accompaniment has a vocational dimension.

Pope Francis has suggested the Global Compact on Education to try and revive commitment in this area. Do you agree with his diagnosis that we now have an educational crisis?

The Society of Jesus completely agrees that there is a huge educational deficit all over the world. Societies today are not offering enough educational opportunities for everyone, and the opportunities that are available are not of a good enough quality. This is a serious problem. Everyone understands that if children are malnourished, they have no future. Exactly the same is true of education. If, as well as providing food and healthcare, society fails to offer you opportunities for self-development and maturation in all areas of life, you will have no future. All serious indicators associate poverty with the lack of a good education. If you are poor, a woman, and you have not received a good education, you are at the bottom of the social scale. Just as we worry about renewable energy and food waste, we should also want to ensure that everyone can access a good-quality education.

Where have you sensed this educational crisis the most?

A few years ago, shortly after my election as Superior General, I made a visit to Nairobi, where I met a group of refugees who came from South Sudan. I was struck by something an 18-year-old girl said to me. She begged the Society of Jesus not to stop offering education in refugee camps. Her question to me was: If young refugees don't receive an education while they are in the camps, when will they do so? She was quite worried about the kind of future they would have without an education. In Africa and the Middle East, people can stay in a refugee camp for up to 15 years. If a boy arrives at a camp when he's 10 and leaves when he is 25 or 30 years old, without having received an education, what will be his future be like? Millions of people are in that situation.

The same thing happens on the fringes of society: there are a lot of people who have no chance at all to access an education. This is one the challenges that the human race as a whole should be addressing. And it is not only a problem about who pays for this education. We also have to look for the means of making it possible. Quality education is really a necessity—and it is the right of every person, every boy or girl who comes into this world.

Political parties tend to change their educational policy when they reach power. Is there a widespread lack of long-term vision for building lasting national educational pacts? How could this tendency be reversed?

That depends on how you envision education. If you see it as an instrument of political ideology, then it is a fight to the death. That is what ideologically motivated regimes do: they seek to impose an ideology on society. That's why, for them, education and propaganda are what count most. That is what happens with exaggerated forms of nationalism that try to re-write history like this. On the other hand, if you view education as a process of maturation in freedom, then your perspective changes completely.

The best example of this can be seen in universities. They lose their essence when they stop being a space for plurality where different ideas can co-exist side-by-side. If society does not reach consensus on a shared social project that is for the good of everyone, then polarization will develop and so will conflicts and fights to control education and the media. That does not mean that there should not be left- or right-wing newspapers or university academics supporting one position or another. What impoverishes society is the imposition of a single way of thinking that cancels out the co-existence of different ideas. Educational systems are quite a good reflection of society: if there is no plurality in the lecture halls, it means there is none out in the streets either. That is one of the reasons why the Society is present in the field of education.

"HE WAS STUDYING WITH THE BOYS, FOLLOWING THE STRUCTURE AND METHOD OF PARIS" [AU 73]

Following the frustration of his desire to remain in Jerusalem, and once he had arrived in Barcelona, Ignatius decided he should study. He did so for two years in Barcelona and then moved to Alcala de Henares to study arts [Au 56]. In Alcala, he was occupied in giving the exercises and "in explaining Christian doctrine" (Au 57), which yielded much fruit. His ability to attract crowds through his preaching drew the attention of the inquisitors. They could not discover any heresy in his teaching but asked him not to speak of things of the faith for the next four years, i.e., until he had finished his studies [Au 62]. This disquieted Ignatius as he did not want to stop speaking of the things of God and, through this, help souls. He went to Salamanca where something similar happened to him. He had problems because he roamed around speaking of God but had not studied theology. In the end he was banned only from speaking about the difference between mortal and venial sin [Au 68], but to Ignatius that small ban felt like a great impediment. He went to Paris. Upon arriving there, he discovered that "he was very lacking in background; he was studying with the boys following the structure and method of Paris" [Au 73]. His immense desire to help souls made him willing to study with the boys, in order to acquire the foundation he needed to speak of the things of God to others. This is one of the most unusual scenes from the life of Ignatius: he, a 36-year-old man, sitting in a classroom with little boys learning Latin, so that he would be able to study at university later. Years later, he would say to Jesuit students: "However, when the study is directed purely to God's service, it is an excellent form of devotion." In the Constitutions he affirmed that it would be "necessary to provide for the edifice of learning, and of skill in employing it, so as to help make God our Creator and Lord better known and served" [Co 307].

PRAYER POINTS

Composition of place. Remember the people and places who were important in my educational process.

Grace to ask for. Lord, may I accept with depth and creativity invitations to commit to the education of those around me, especially those most in need.

First point. Dwell on the educational needs of the children, teenagers, and young people where I live. Reflect on this and draw spiritual profit from it.

Second point. Imagine the opportunities and benefits that children, teenagers, and young people could receive if we offer them the education they need.

BIBLE TEXTS

» **Luke 24:13–35.** Education allows us to interpret the meaning of events, just as Jesus helped the disciples understand what happened on the road to Emmaus. How can I help ensure that education leads to an increase in critical thinking, a desire for truth, and the joy of the proclamation of true life?

» **Mark 9:33–37.** How can a Jesuit education help children, teenagers, and young people draw close to Jesus, to other people, and to creation?

» **Luke 18:15–17.** Depth and the ability to discern and the search for the common good are, among other things, features of the kind of education the Society of Jesus wishes to offer. Do our educational pathways lead us to this or are we being called to something more?

Colloquy. Like a friend chatting with another friend, tell Jesus, as though you were a disciple on the Road to Emmaus, of your dreams and hopes, your questions and desires for the education of young people and children. End with an Our Father and a Hail Mary. Do not forget to examine what has come up during the prayer time.

TIPS FOR SPIRITUAL CONVERSATION

For spiritual conversation that arises from personal prayer, the following steps from the general methodology of spiritual conversation are recommended (p. 268).

For spiritual conversation concerning an apostolic work, the following prayer points may be beneficial.

Composition of place. Bring to mind the many stories you know of communities and individuals who have overcome their problems thanks to education.

Grace to ask for. Lord, may I know that I am called by you to commit myself to education wherever I may find myself on mission.

Bible text. Luke 24:13–35. Do we promote good-quality education in our apostolic works and missions? Do we foster critical thought and depth as paths towards the truth, and commitment to solidarity and fraternity? Are we being asked to do something more? To which challenges does the Lord invite us to respond?

Colloquy. Like a friend chatting with another friend, tell Jesus, as though you were a disciple on the road to Emmaus, of your dreams and hopes, your uncertainties and longings regarding the education of the youngest children of all. End with an Our Father and a Hail Mary. Do not forget to examine what you have experienced during the prayer time. The fruit of this may be shared according to the steps of general methodology for Spiritual Conversation.

The Society of Jesus has always worked with companions on the mission. In the 16th century, for example, the laypeople who helped the Jesuits were essential to their work in North America. The same was true for Matteo Ricci in China. Over the course of time, the order has received invaluable help from their companions and partners on the mission. That tradition continues today, with the adoption of new methods to respond to our changing times.

11 The Shared Mission: Lessons in Dialogue and Openness

Pentecost. Alejandro Labajos, SJ

How would you define the shared mission? Does it go any further than a straightforward partnership with laypeople?

Jesuits are partners on a mission which is not ours but belongs to Christ. That has always been the case, and it springs from our surrender to the Church, which itself was established to continue the mission of Christ. Paul VI's Apostolic Exhortation *Evangelii Nuntiandi* states very clearly that the Church's raison d'être is evangelisation.

> **Jesuits are partners on a mission that is not ours, but belongs to Christ.**

The Society of Jesus developed to serve the Church. This is emphasized in the Universal Apostolic Preferences and has many consequences for our order. Knowing, as Ignatius and his first companions did, that it is "the least Society" is a hallmark of our identity. The idea of being the least is nothing to do with numbers. It means that the Society is subordinate to something larger: the Church and her mission. This is an Ignatian way of understanding humility. Jesuits should be aware that this is our raison d'être.

How did the idea of the shared mission emerge in the Society of Jesus?

In Spain they use the expression *shared mission*, while in Latin America the phrase *companions on the mission* is more widely deployed, and the Anglophone world speaks of *partners in mission*. Whichever term is used, the meaning is always the same: we are partners in the mission of Christ. As companions who are called to be with him, we share the responsibility of making present the good news of the Gospel.

We should, however, watch out for a potential danger in regard to this: are we allowing laypeople to share our mission? Or are we the ones placing ourselves at the service of others? This is a shared mission because it is for the whole Church and all of us are the People of God. This is not about whether or not we have partners but seeing how we can partner with others. That change of emphasis should also affect how we understand the partnerships we have. We must share the mission of the Society of Jesus but at the same time partner with projects outside the Society that are not necessarily ours. In China, for example, The Beijing Center (TBC) is located within the campus of the University of International Business and Economics (UIBE), with whom it has a very positive relationship. Many other examples along similar lines, which go well beyond opening Jesuit projects to partnerships with other people, could also be cited.

This is about seeing how we can partner with others.

What kind of impact did the Second Vatican Council have on this area?

The Council emphasized that the Church should be understood as the People of God, which obliged a rethink of the role of religious life, including that of the Society of Jesus. It made it quite clear that those who are consecrated are not part of the hierarchy and that we have a role as collaborators within the Church. We embody a singular category within the People of God because we consecrate our lives specifically to the mission of the Church. Obviously, religious congregations in the Church include many orders whose members are mainly priests, but ordained religious have always sought to retain an identity that is distinct from that of the diocesan priest. Although we may do the same things as ordained diocesan priests, we do so drawing on our own charism as religious. Our identity as religious helps us carry out our priestly ministry as a service to the People of God. The life of religious is collaborative within the community that is the Church and is at the service of its mission.

How is the shared mission developed in the works instigated by the Jesuits?

That is where the dynamic can change and the idea of a Jesuit being a partner on the mission can get a little blurred, because many might argue that at the end of the day, it is the Jesuit who should make the decisions. This was even more the case in the first half of the 20th century, when our apostolic works were in the main run by Jesuits. Only those on the fringes were really open to partnerships. However, in the past 50 years, an understanding has gradually developed that apostolic works may be jointly run and that what defines them is their identity, not the number of Jesuits involved nor the positions they may hold within them. This has not been an easy transition, neither can it be said to be complete yet. Truly sharing the management of our projects with others has not proved to be that straightforward. It happened initially because the numbers of Jesuits were decreasing and because our activities were increasing. We had to fight against an attitude of employing people just to do the jobs Jesuits were no longer able to do, in order to adopt a new mentality and embrace very different working relationships, namely ones in which we accept non-Jesuits who work with us as fellow companions on our mission.

This is not about having non-Jesuit partners in the Society's apostolic mission but about having coworkers on the mission which belongs to Christ, not the Society. A shared mission is not the consequence of a fall in Jesuit vocations but rather part of the apostolic essence of the Church. Shifting from the first idea to the second has been a big step and means that, by implication, we partner with people familiar with the identity of our works and who feel called to share in serving the mission of Christ in the Church.

The past three General Congregations have stressed the importance of shared mission. How has this area developed?

It's been a fascinating process. After GC32 (1975) there was a trend to make laypeople associates of the Society, even in juridical terms. GC33 (1983) approved this *ad experimentum*, and interesting initiatives with lay associations began to develop in various countries. That sparked a key debate at GC34 (1995), where it became clear that this was not the way ahead, as laypeople should continue to be laypeople and not turn into semi-religious. Everyone involved in our mission should partner with it by drawing on their own vocation. That was how we ended up establishing a new kind of relationship, which has developed further over the past 25 years. This involves sharing our identity and charism, which we convey by offering our collaborators a journey of spiritual experience. The change in the Society in the past quarter century has been massive. In some provinces, the majority of our apostolic works are directed today by laypeople, especially by women who enrich the way the mission develops.

How has the Society changed through the inclusion of laypeople in decision-making roles and partnership with other religious?

It has changed a great deal, both in its public image and in how it is managed, because a new way of advancing our apostolic works has emerged, which has enriched our spirituality and the way we relate to each other. It is a stimulating way to run the mission. Some works have emerged from this spirit of partnership, such as Fe y Alegría, which only ever involved a few Jesuits. Indeed, partnership is one of its key features. At the start, this involved primarily religious, but gradually laymen and laywomen became involved. Today, the vast majority of those in charge of this huge project are laypeople.

The same could be said of the Jesuit Refugee Service (JRS). It was never intended to be a project run mainly by the Jesuits. Today it operates thanks to countless laypeople, male and female, and non-Jesuit religious and diocesan priests who partner in the mission. Another example of collaboration is the Christian Life Community (CLC), which is not, strictly speaking, an apostolic work but a lay community. Since the Second Vatican Council, the CLC has grown and matured as a lay organization. Its lay leaders are responsible for running the CLC. The Society of Jesus partners with CLC by offering spiritual accompaniment but is not involved in any way in managing the organization. This is a journey on which we are learning how to provide a setting that allows each person to develop their own vocation and independent management style. It is also about ensuring that we can connect when the time comes for us to share responsibility for the mission or through spiritual accompaniment.

People are now referred to as companions on the mission rather than mission partners. What does this change of wording imply?
The change in terminology is really significant. It reflects the depth of our decision to journey together. Using the term *companions on the mission* makes it clear that this involves people who decide to join a shared mission. They are not simply rendering a professional service but go further by sharing in the meaning of the apostolic work, its identity, sources of inspiration, and all, in short, that sharing a mission entails. This question elicited great debate in Latin America at the end of the 90s, when people began to speak of the apostolic body, which they thought was formed as much by Jesuits as by their companions on the mission.

What are the risks and opportunities of shared mission work?
The greatest risk is loss of identity. This can happen to the point that the word *Jesuit* in the title is the only thing that remains Jesuit in a given ministry, but it no longer has any apostolic impact in the sense intended by the Society. There is a tremendous responsibility of creating the means and ways for this identity to be shared so that institutions have processes in place to maintain this identity. It's a big challenge.

When there were greater numbers of Jesuits, the identity of our institutions was absorbed by osmosis. Now, in contrast, this has to be fostered in a deliberate and systematic fashion. The process adopted by the 27 universities that are the responsibility of the Society in the United States is very interesting. They have undertaken an examen, in the Ignatian sense of the word, concerning the identity and mission of each one via a process of self-evaluation and heteroevaluation. This concluded with recommendations on how to preserve our identity, which are included in strategic plans, in order to ensure that they are put into practice and continually evaluated. The Union of Jesuit Universities in Spain (UNIJES) is heading in the same direction, and the Fe y Alegría network has similar initiatives underway. Our experience tells us that the key to ensuring that our identity is retained and communicated effectively is to have our institutions work together in a network.

How much is the decreasing number of Jesuits and number of ageing Jesuits a factor in following this collaborative route?

Certainly, the declining number of Jesuits has been an important factor in raising our awareness of this, but it's not really the main reason. What has proved far more influential has been understanding the mission of the Society according to the ecclesiology of Vatican II, i.e., the Church being a community of communities in which all share responsibility for the mission, according to their specific vocations and charisms.

When the numbers of Jesuits began to decline, we had two options. The first was to reduce the number of activities we ran in proportion to the number of Jesuits available to run them. The other was to follow the path of sharing the mission, which is what has happened in the Society in the main. In Spain, for instance, the order now has far more schools than it did when it had more members there. In another context, the United States, we have had to maintain 27 universities with only a third of the Jesuits who were around several years ago. This has led to us needing to take big steps over a short period of time. The first lay President of a Jesuit university was nominated barely 20 years ago, at Georgetown University in Washington, D.C. Today, half our university presidents are laymen or laywomen. This percentage is higher when it comes to roles such as Vice-Rector, Dean, Director, etc. In Europe and other places, this is increasingly the case, mainly in educational settings. In fidelity to the Second Vatican Council, we have been learning to adopt a broader approach and to do things together. This yields great fruit in apostolic terms.

Why was shared mission named as a principle that applies across all the Universal Apostolic Preferences?

The last General Congregation stated that partnership, working as a network, and discernment were all areas that should be taken into account in all the Universal Apostolic Preferences, because they constitute aspects of our modus operandi. During this process, a certain—at times very human—reluctance has emerged regarding whether or not we share power and make the final decisions on management. Are we prepared to not have the last word? Obviously, this is a complex question in big institutions while having an impact on small ones.

What have you personally learnt from the shared mission? Where has it made the most progress?

I have learnt a lot. For me, it has been a continuing lesson in dialogue, in opening up to what is new, and becoming ripe for discovery in other people and their experiences. For the Society, it has been a tremendous asset. Progress happens at the pace of the setting of each apostolic work. With partnerships, the Ignatian principle of adapting to times, places, and people to be more efficient in mission, also must apply. However, there is no general parameter by which we measure advances and setbacks. Each situation always needs to be discerned on an individual basis.

Your mission partnerships involve other religious congregations, especially female ones. How can joint projects among the institutions of female religious in the Ignatian family be further strengthened?

This is a path we are also learning about as we go along. In light of falling vocations, a tension arises between starting out on new pathways or giving in to the temptation to withdraw to the path on which we feel most at home. I recall that after the Conferences of the Latin American Bishops in Medellin (1968) and Puebla (1979), some female religious congregations gave over their schools so they could join the Fe y Alegría network. Another trend has been to form a group within each congregation who takes charge of running the apostolic works that until now were carried out exclusively by members of that congregation.

Deepening collaboration between religious congregations is always an ongoing task. It involves conquering the fear of losing a charism or a way of understanding the congregation's identity that may lead us to cling to whatever remains instead of opening up to new ways of managing our apostolic works through collaboration. If we understand that charisms exist to enrich the Church, the People of God, and have no meaning in themselves alone, we will understand that not only do they have to be renounced because we are managing apostolic projects in partnership, but that we should create the optimum conditions for all members of the one body in mission, whose head is Christ, to be enriched.

How do laypeople help prevent the Society of Jesus from sliding into self-centredness and clericalism?

They're a good vaccine against those tendencies, which are always there, like a massive temptation. They allow us to discover that in the mission of the Church there is room for everyone to exist and to express themselves, according to their individual vocation. That is absolutely necessary if the Church that Vatican II dreamt of, the People of God on the move thanks to the diverse charisms of the Holy Spirit, is to become a reality.

Does the idea of spiritual conversion, the theme of the Ignatian year, need to be adapted to laypeople?

Don't forget that Ignatius had his conversion as a layperson. His spiritual process began when he discovered his vocation as a Christian, that Christ was at the center of his life as a layperson and his apostolate through the conversations and the Spiritual Exercises. It is a process we can all experience at some point in our lives. In this sense, the call to conversion is by no means exclusive to religious or priests. It is universal and applies to the whole Church. Conversion means turning our gaze to Christ, allowing him to show us the way, that he may reaffirm us in our individual vocation and lead us to a greater depth and commitment to him, to ourselves, to others, and creation. Rather than adapting the idea of conversion to laypeople, as religious, whether male or female or priests, we should accompany laypeople in the discovery of the call to conversion that God awakens in their individual vocations.

Perhaps part of our conversion as priests and religious is to trust in the ability of laypeople to discern their particular callings and experience deep processes of conversion. Rather than adapting the concept of conversion to laypeople, they need to be offered the tools of Ignatian spirituality so that they can undergo their own individual process. We need to stop seeing laypeople as being underage in terms of the faith. They have just as much or more ability than we do to develop a committed and adult faith. Listening, accompanying, trusting… perhaps that is the conversion that God is calling us to as Jesuits.

Can a work of the Society of Jesus be run only by laypeople? How does the Society offer formation and support to laypeople in leadership roles?

Not only can laypeople do this, in quite a few institutions they are already doing this. Thank God, this is a growing trend. The challenge is how to accompany the laypeople who are part of the Apostolic body of the Society. Experiences of this are many and multi-faceted. First of all, we need to consider the professional competence of the person running the institution. We need to build competencies to do this. The next step is getting to know the person concerned and find out why they want to work here and not somewhere else. That is linked to the experience of Ignatian spirituality. That is why in all our programs, the experience of the Spiritual Exercises and accompaniment in the Ignatian sense of the word is only gradually introduced.

Little by little we are learning to deliver this process better so that everyone can access a good, properly delivered experience of accompaniment. This is not something that only Jesuits can offer laypeople; laypeople can be excellent companions. Many Jesuits are accompanied by laypeople.

How does the Society of Jesus form its members so that they are prepared to work on shared mission?

Nowadays, it's very common for laymen, laywomen, and female religious to accompany Spiritual Exercises for the Jesuits, either individually or in a group. This is very enriching. I know some Jesuits whose spiritual directors are laymen, laywomen, or religious with longstanding experience. Members of the Society, who in the past were formed only with other Jesuits, today receive their formation right from the start alongside non-Jesuit formators and guides. This is a great asset and very helpful in the apostolate, where having to work with others is a simple fact. However, there are still Jesuits who struggle with being sent to an organisation where they have to receive orders from a lay director. Being a Jesuit is not about being "the son of the owner" but just another servant in the mission of the Lord.

If a layperson and a Jesuit can both do the same job, what is the difference between them?

Nothing, if one wants to differentiate between them on the grounds of what they do. If both teach math or are in charge of the administration of a school, in terms of efficiency or professionalism, there is no reason for there to be any difference at all. The difference comes from who they are, not what they do. The difference comes from the specific vocation that each is called to. The Jesuit is consecrated through vows that invite him to love without ties, detach from material goods, and be open to being sent anywhere, according to the needs of the mission. The vocation to religious consecration enriches the Church via a huge diversity of charisms that complement the lay vocation and ordination to Holy Orders. Without laypeople, there is no Church. They form the foundation of the body, which gathers to follow Jesus and continue his mission throughout history. A layperson lives out their Christian life in every sphere of human activity, doing as many things as their gifts allow, for the mission of the Lord.

What distinguishes what is Ignatian from what is Jesuit?

The word *Jesuitical* or *Jesuit* is understood to mean someone or something whose ultimate authority, including in legal and financial terms, is the Society of Jesus. The meaning of Ignatian is more to do with inspiration and usually refers to a style of educating or a spirituality. There are quite a few female religious congregations that are Ignatian because their founders were inspired by the style of religious life and occasionally also by the Constitutions of Ignatius of Loyola. There are also Ignatian schools that do not belong to the Society, although some are connected to it via collaborative networks.

You took part in the Youth Synod. What did you think of the presence of women in these meetings?

Their presence was very enriching. Overall, they were young and audacious women who gave the meeting a special tone. With the Synod, there was a deep conceptual debate surrounding the presence of women. I think that in the future, things could be reformed so that more options are available and so that we gain a better understanding of the idea of a Synodal Church. But, at the same time, it makes sense for the Bishops to meet together and that there should be spaces that are not open to everyone. Furthermore, the Synod of Bishops is a consultative body and does not make decisions. The Pope could in future promote a consultative body that represents the whole People of God. This would be an outcome of the ecclesiology of the Second Vatican Council.

However, we should remember that although only the bishops vote, the assemblies of the Synod of Bishops that have taken place in the past 10 years have been the fruit of very broad participatory processes. At the grassroots level, this includes the faithful who raise their concerns via parishes, movements, and schools. I recall for instance that one year before the Amazon Synod, during a visit to the Bolivian region of Moxos, I met a group of around 50 indigenous people who were preparing for the Synodal Assembly. Some of them travelled later on to Rome. While it's true that it's the Pope who speaks after the Synod, he does so after listening to a diverse range of voices over a long period of time.

What has it been like for you personally to work with women who hold positions of responsibility in the Society of Jesus?
Well, I'll give you two examples. When I was the provincial in Venezuela, I set up a commission for apostolic planning whose main advisor was a laywoman. She determined how we designed the planning. During the 10 years I was Rector of the Catholic University of Táchira, the administrative vice-rector

was a very competent woman who managed to increase the university's rather slender resources. Women are excellent administrators, and they administrate without being tight-fisted, ensuring that everyone receives just what they need without any unnecessary expenditure. I have also noticed that they have no problem telling you when something can't be done and have creativity to spare when it comes to finding new ways to obtain what is needed.

What do you think of the request, voiced by some Catholics, for women to join the priesthood? Would the female diaconate be a good idea?

Both topics generate debates in the Church that can be easily contaminated by other issues in society, including the journey towards female equality. Our debate should stick to looking at what the Church is and what it wants to be. I have always shared my life as a Christian with women and see it as very normal for women to organize and lead grassroots communities through prayer, catechesis, and the daily sharing of the Word. Without women, there would be no community life. This always happened in a very natural way in my milieu without anyone saying they needed to be ordained a deacon. I do think, however, that the idea of diaconal female ministry needs proper study. The Pope has asked for guidance regarding this from theologians and other experts. Hopefully they will enlighten us. However, what seems much clearer to me is that we should not try to clericalize laypeople, whether men or women, but should develop the mission of laypeople in the Church in order to offer a more diverse pastoral service.

*Do you think those who argue that the institutional Church is a
sexist organisation are in any degree correct?*

The Church develops in specific cultural contexts and, in a
sense, replicates scenarios from these contexts. It might be said,
for instance, that St. Paul was pro-slavery because he did not
fight for the freedom of slaves, who were part of his culture.
However, Paul introduced a fundamental concept that destroyed
all forms of slavery within us and all unjust inequality when he
wrote to the Galatians that: "all of you who were baptized into
Christ have clothed yourselves with Christ. There is neither Jew
nor Gentile, neither slave nor free, nor is there male and female,
for you are all one in Christ Jesus… If you belong to Christ,
then you are Abraham's seed, and heirs according to the promise." Later he tells them that "it is for freedom that Christ has
set us free," thus going deeper into the meaning of this freedom,
which Jesus rooted in love and which surpasses even the law in
all its forms.

Something similar applies with the role of women in the
Church: it has been shaped according to the culture in which
the Church has developed, and yet the history of the Church
has always included individuals who have recalled this fundamental equity and liberty. We need to remember this. Accusing
the Church of being sexist in a society that is sexist takes things
out of context, although it certainly does not mean that nothing
should be done about this. If I may speak for a moment of my
own experience in Latin America, where the presence of women
is fundamental, I was not taught to pray by priests but by the
women in my family. Who nourishes the faith of communities?
In the vast majority of cases, women. They have a huge role in

the Church, far beyond the fact they are not allowed to take Holy Orders. However, it needs to be stated categorically that we are not satisfied with the situation of women in the Church.

How is the Society of Jesus trying to place women at the heart of things and give them prominence?

General Congregation 34 discerned a call to pass a decree on the Society and the situation of women in the Church and in society. Among other things, this encouraged Jesuits to listen to women attentively, in a spirit of partnership and equality, as a proviso for not dismissing their real concerns, and getting over attitudes of condescension and male dominance. This put in place the practical and effective basis of our mutual partnership for the reformation of unjust structures. Today in the Society there are many women in roles of responsibility. The majority are school principals or are in leadership roles in the educational sphere. They are an increasing presence too in centers of spirituality, where they give the Exercises and accompany people doing them. But there is still more to be accomplished.

We have created an international commission to explore the role of women in the Society to go deeper into this issue. The impetus for this working group came from the last meeting of the Social Secretariat: 40 percent of those present were women. In that meeting I set out 10 points to examine with transparency and courage how we conduct the social and environmental dimension of our mission. One point asked that we review the place of women in our institutions and social priorities, in our processes of discernment, and in decision making in our life and mission. Another recommendation was that we look at the place and the priority given to the challenges faced by women in a world that marginalizes or excludes them and in a Church reluctant to acknowledge their co-responsibility in leading the community of Christ's followers. As a result of the presentation, the women attending the meeting asked to meet with me, and we had a conversation out of which emerged the idea of creating this commission, which should soon bear fruit.

In the mission are there possibilities for partnership with people of other religions, or who are agnostic or atheists?

There is a point on which we all agree, which is the idea of humanity. This is happening even more noticeably after the encyclical *Fratelli Tutti*. This partnership is based on the fact that we are all human and we can dialogue, show solidarity with one another, serve others, take charge of crisis situations, build a better society, and take care of the environment. Exploring things on a human level opens a space for collaboration.

The mystery of the Incarnation is about God taking on the human condition. It embraces all of us, inviting us to collaborate with people of all religions: with Hindus in India, with Muslims in Africa and Indonesia, with Buddhists in Japan, Cambodia, Myanmar, and Sri Lanka, etc. We are called to partner even with those of no religious belief. In general terms, we are called in fact to partner with all people of good will. Divisions based on religion or race, and intolerance towards those of other beliefs or religious practices, are attacks on humanity in a world that is becoming ever more fundamentalist.

How does the shared mission complement the Jesuits' efforts to create networks? Which institutions are these networks developing with? And what does this mean today for the Society of Jesus?
Our shared mission and the networks are mutually complementary. Sharing the mission is a way of developing the Society's modus operandi. The work we do via the networks is another way of working together, one that offers many benefits with regard to the use of resources. I spoke earlier of my experience while I was Rector of the Catholic University of Táchira, a relatively small institution in an isolated region. Being able to join the network of Latin American universities gave the university a broader dimension, one previously quite inconceivable. The same is true of Fe y Alegría, which began initially as a series of schools and that subsequently linked together in a network so that they could develop a shared identity. Each of the Society's schools was established on an individual basis, and today they belong to various international networks. The universities entrusted to the Society of Jesus function in regional networks and in 2018 created an international association that operate via a network.

Such processes are becoming increasingly fruitful and productive, enriching the way we work, thanks to the emergence of new technological resources. This has happened at every level in our educational activities, in our social work, and in our centers of spirituality. All kinds of apostolic initiatives are now making the most of this. Operating as a network leads us to get involved with other people, which naturally broadens our horizons. This is a reality that multiplies the possibilities.

What are the biggest hurdles and hesitations that need to be overcome in the networks? How does the Society of Jesus organize this?

Any process of transformation evokes reluctance because it's hard to change our way of doing things. That's completely normal. The greatest hurdle comes from the need to find another way of organizing the use of our time and energy. Working in a network requires time and resources. It is not something that can be done in isolation. It entails a new way of relating to institutions, students, and people in general. That's why we need to exchange our way of thinking for a mentality that's more productive. In the Society of Jesus up until now, the work in networks has been organized from the bottom up, without being coordinated at a global level. In some cases, over time, greater coordination has been necessary, but always within a context of respect for how the networks interact. I don't really imagine that everything can be centralized.

"THEN I ALONE, WHAT CAN I BE?" [EX 58]

"In his day, St. Ignatius gave shelter to the homeless of Rome, cared for prostitutes, and established homes for orphans. He sought collaborators and with them established organizations and networks to continue these and many other forms of service. To respond today to the pressing needs of our complex and fragile world, many hands are surely needed. Collaboration in mission is the way we respond to this situation: it expresses our true identity as members of the Church, the complementarity of our diverse calls to holiness, our mutual responsibility for the mission of Christ, our desire to join people of good will in the service of the human family, and the coming of the Kingdom of God. It is a grace given to us in this moment, one consistent with our Jesuit way of proceeding."[19]

PRAYER POINTS

Composition of place. Imagine some of the initiatives in which Jesuits, laypeople, religious, and other people of good will could work together to produce fruit for the mission of Christ.

Grace to ask for. Lord, help me use the gifts you have given me to partner with your mission at this particular time.

First point. Consider how your life is supported by and entwines with that of countless people who give of their gifts and talents so that this world may more closely resemble the Kingdom of God. Reflect on this and reap spiritual profit.

Second point. Remember with gratitude the names of all those people of varying walks of life and vocations who have offered their resources, time, and gifts so that the mission may be fulfilled. Reflect on this and reap spiritual profit.

---

19 CG 35, d. 6, n. 213.

BIBLE TEXTS

» **Matthew 25:14–30.** We are called to use through our actions whatever the Lord has given us. Which gifts and talents has the Lord given you? How are you using them to partner with God in whichever place you are in? Do you welcome with joy and a spirit of openness the gifts and offerings of others in the context of the mission? If so, why?

» **Matthew 21:28–32.** Both reluctance and willingness come up when we partner with others. Collaboration involves a process during which we allow ourselves to be persuaded that working with others will take all of us further. Our gifts are complementary, so if we use them together, they will yield more fruit. What kind of reluctance to working with others comes up in you? How has a readiness to share in mission grown within you? How would you describe the fruit that comes forth during a process of partnership?

Colloquy. In his speech to General Congregation 36, Pope Francis stated: "We walk neither by ourselves nor for our own comfort."[20] Dialogue with the Lord, the one we partner with on our mission, and let him tell you of his dreams and longings for this world and how you can partner with him so that they gradually be-come real in the course of time. End with an Our Father and a Hail Mary. Do not forget to examine what you have experienced during the prayer time.

---

20 Pope Francis, Speech to the members of the 36th General Congregation of the Society of Jesus, Rome, October 24th, 2016. See: https://bit.ly/3tmk2qE.

TIPS FOR SPIRITUAL CONVERSATION

For spiritual conversation that arises from personal prayer, the following steps from the general methodology of spiritual conversation are recommended (p. 268).

For spiritual conversation concerning an apostolic work, the following prayer points may be beneficial.

Composition of place. Imagine some of the initiatives in which Jesuits, laypeople, the religious, and other people of good will partner together and yield fruit for the mission of Christ.

Grace to ask for. Lord help me use the gifts you have given me to partner with your mission wherever I am.

Bible text. Mark 9:38–40. Within our own apostolic work, are we open to working with others? Who are we willing to partner with so that our works may yield more fruit for the Kingdom? Do we have enough courage to learn from others, even the least among us? Do we create the space and time for collaboration, for meeting and searching for a shared horizon in our mission? Do we fall into the temptation of self-sufficiency, or are we open to interdependence? What helps yield greater apostolic fruitfulness and serves for the greater glory of God?

Colloquy. Speak and listen to the Lord, with whose mission we partner. Allow him to tell you about his dreams and longings for this world and how you can partner with him on your mission and in your apostolic work so that these dreams and longings become a reality in our world. End with an Our Father and a Hail Mary. Do not forget to examine what has come up during the prayer. The fruits of the prayer time may be shared according to the steps for the general methodology of Spiritual Conversation.

Final Thoughts

Fr. Arturo Sosa with Darío Menor. Photograph by Robert Ballecer, SJ

Some conversations strip you bare; they invite you to stop, look inside yourself, evaluate what you find, and reflect on what might be better if you changed things. They are dialogues which, to put this in Jesuit vocabulary, kindle discernment. That was the impact on me of 24 hours of one-to-one interviews with Arturo Sosa, the Superior General of the Society of Jesus. The transcription of those conversations, contained in these pages, led to *Walking with Ignatius*. They may not leave the reader unscathed either.

The celebration of the Ignatian Year, held to mark the 500th anniversary of the wound that the young Íñigo of Loyola suffered in Pamplona and which sparked his conversion, led the Curia General of the Jesuits to champion the publication of this book. It is largely the result of 11 interviews which Fr. Sosa gave this journalist in Rome during the final months of 2020. While the world was locked in the grip of Coronavirus, we shut ourselves away to chat in room 330 of the Jesuits' ancient building in Borgo Santo Spirito, the headquarters of the Catholic Church's largest male congregation.

The first successor of St. Ignatius to hail from Latin America responded to around 270 questions. His replies analyzed the situation of the world, the Church, and the Society of Jesus, as well as the big challenges his order is addressing, as outlined in the Universal Apostolic Preferences. But above all, Sosa unpacked the need for conversion in various areas of life, an idea that goes way beyond individual religious convictions by challenging us to place our personal fears, hopes, and preconceived ideas under the microscope. The aim of this process, which is by no means easy, is to come out the other end a better person who focuses on other people rather than ourselves. This is so necessary in a time like ours, when a large part of the world is in the throes of individualism and self-absorption.

The process of preparing *Walking with Ignatius* for publication, however, was not limited to a journalist asking questions and Fr. Sosa providing informative, analytical answers and opinions. It started a process of joint reflection with other members of the Society of Jesus. Thus, the aim is to invite the reader on a journey of conversion which will lead them not to see the world only with fear or a fur-rowed brow but to develop an openness towards the action of God, working with others, and caring for the environment.

Walking with Ignatius thus aspires to be a kind of handbook, a set of pages for the reader to dip into for suggestions on how to experience in depth the Ignatian Year held between May 20, 2021 and July 31, 2022. Its motto is "Seeing anew all things in Christ." This book also provides an in-depth under-standing of what drives the Society of Jesus today. Probably the most influential religious order of the last half millennium of Church history, the Jesuits have been in the spotlight anew since 2013, when Jorge Mario Bergoglio became the first son of Ignatius to be elected Pope. The pontificate of Francis cannot be understood without an awareness of its profoundly Jesuit hallmark.

These pages also offer an introduction to the ideas and character of Arturo Sosa, 31st Superior General of the Society of Jesus. A Venezuelan with a genial smile under his distinctive white moustache, he is a man open to God and to the world. He is a confirmed optimist. "Happiness is what human life means at its deepest level. God created us to be happy," he says. This is not a naive or unwarranted optimism. It is rather the fruit of his faith and his firm belief that Jesus "will be with us every day until the end of time." That quotation from the Gospel of Mark is seared on Sosa's conscience.

With the broad outlook he has acquired through his personality, formation, and role, the Jesuit leader expresses in this book his concept of the Church, arising from an awareness that, as the Second Vatican Council explains, it is essentially the People of God on the move. That is the source of his commitment to sharing mission with the laity and his firm rejection of clericalism, which he regards as a "kind of ecclesial populism." This also explains his broad take on secularisation which helps us distinguish between authentic experiences of God and religion lived out as a societal habit, or even as an ideology.

Sosa combines the universality inherent in his Catholic identity and vocation as Jesuit with a profound love for his native Venezuela, a nation whose plight makes him weep "with sorrow." Even before his election in 2016 as a successor to St. Ignatius, he had extensive experience as a social and political analyst. This outlook he has broadened further still since becoming Superior General. His role offers him "privileged access to a great deal of information in places with a Jesuit presence." That is a large swathe of the world, given that the approximately 15,000 members of the Society of Jesus operate in 127 countries, or 65 percent of those on the whole planet.

This is the vision behind Sosa's constructive analysis of the major crises facing humanity today, including the consequences of the pandemic and the environmental emergency caused by an unjust socio-economic system that causes poverty, inequality, and deprivation. *Walking with Ignatius* explains how the Jesuits try to respond to the cry of refugees, immigrants, and other vulnerable groups while at the same time endeavouring to promote change via education. They also champion leadership, boldness, and people's political identity, all key factors in achieving a true conversion today, whether on a personal level or in society as a whole.

For the author, it has been both a privilege and a bracing pleasure to be in dialogue for so many hours with Arturo Sosa. I am profoundly grateful for this opportunity, which has given me the chance, admittedly rare for a news journalist, to forget the usual pressures and time-constraints of my profession and talk and reflect at leisure about life's big questions. My thanks likewise are due to the team at the General Curia of the Society of Jesus, for their unfailing patience, advice, and support.

Darío Menor

Rome, January 2021

TIPS FOR SPIRITUAL CONVERSATION

Methodology:

These are three of the basic elements of spiritual conversation: sharing in depth one's own interior movements (motions or feelings, reactions, intuitions); listening that is open and attentive to the motions of others, allowing their insights to enlighten our own; and the search for shared horizons so that we may embark on a communal journey, inspired by God's individual invitations, which lead us to love more and to serve. Due to this, we recommend three separate steps in times of spiritual conversation.

In a setting of shared prayer:

First, *listening*. Go round the group and share in a simple yet deep way the key insights and invitations that God has made to each person during their personal prayer time. The others in the group should listen attentively to each person speaking without interrupting them with questions or to offer their opinion. Just let what each speaker has experienced shed light on the internal experience of every member of the group. Depending on the size of the community or group, leave a short time of silence between each speaker so that all may "realise and relish interiorly" whatever the speaker has said.

Second, *echoes*. After deeply listening to everyone in the group and allowing for a brief moment of prayerful silence, have another round of spiritual sharing. This one is to allow people to share whatever insights emerged for them as they listened to the sharing of others. The aim is not to evaluate the words of others in the group, or to offer lengthy reflections, but for talking about how the sharing of others has helped shed greater light on our own personal motions, or else how it has sparked an interior movement that has led us towards a greater internal clarity about God's call.

Third, *communion.* After having listened to one another and shared insights, there is a time to look at what everyone's personal calls have in common. The following questions may help with this: Where is the Lord leading us? Which invitations are coming up repeatedly and could be translated into specific community or apostolic actions? What do we need to do to nurture God's call to us as individuals and as a community? This isn't about merely agreeing with one another or reaching a consensus. It is about responding fittingly and generously to the invitation the Spirit is inspiring in the community.

N.B.:

It is key to have a moderator for these times of spiritual conversation who can guide the process and later summarize what has been shared. Pay particular attention to the ambience created for the prayer time; starting and finishing with a text, song, or action may be helpful. It may also help to place a symbolic object in the room used (a light, an icon, a Crucifix, etc.) that can foster the sense of an encounter with the Lord. Also, if it is considered appropriate, to enhance the quality of listening and sharing, the three steps listed above may be split into separate meetings.

Take, O Lord,
and receive my entire liberty,
my memory, my understanding and my whole will.
All that I am and all that I possess,
Thou hast given me:
I surrender it all to Thee to be disposed of according to Thy will.
Give me only Thy love and Thy grace;
with these I will be rich enough and will desire nothing more.
Amen.

St. Ignatius of Loyola

Ignatius, the Pilgrim. Sculpture by William (Bill) McElcheran, Canada